This book belongs to

Sarah

with our love
Jacqueline & Gerry

Grandma's
Special Recipes

Jams, Jellies
& Preserves

hinkler

Published by Hinkler Books Pty Ltd
45–55 Fairchild Street
Heatherton Victoria 3202 Australia
www.hinkler.com.au

hinkler

Design © Hinkler Books Pty Ltd 2012
Food photography and recipe development © StockFood, The Food Media Agency

Cover design: Beverley Gutierrez and Hinkler Design Studio
Stitching, embroidery and screen-printed illustrations created by Beverley Gutierrez
Internal design: Beverley Gutierrez and Hinkler Design Studio
Typesetting: MPS Limited
Prepress: Graphic Print Group

ISBN: 978 1 7430 8474 8

Printed and bound in China

Contents

INTRODUCTION 4–7

CHAPTER ONE 8–39
Jams & Marmalades

CHAPTER TWO 40–69
Jellies & Curds

CHAPTER THREE 70–89
Preserves

CHAPTER FOUR 90–111
Chutneys & Relishes

CHAPTER FIVE 112–133
*Tapenades, Pesto,
Oils & Vinegars*

CHAPTER SIX 134–155
Pickles

WEIGHTS & MEASURES 156

INDEX 157–158

Preserving traditions

In days gone by, families gathered fruits and vegetables in season, preserving them in various ways. These traditions were almost lost but, thankfully, self-sufficiency is back in vogue – partly from a desire for high-quality foods with that unique homemade taste, and partly from a wish to enjoy the traditional pastimes of cooking and preserving.

Popular preserves

Jam is a thick mixture of fruit and sugar, cooked until the pieces of fruit are very soft and almost indistinct.

Marmalade is a clear, jelly-like preserve made from the pulp and rind of fruit, especially citrus fruit.

Jelly is a translucent mixture made from fruit juice, sugar and sometimes pectin. It should be crystal clear and the texture should quiver, but it should hold its shape.

Curd has a soft, smooth texture, which is stiffer and smoother than that of jam. Fruit curds have only short shelf lives because they contain butter and eggs and not as much sugar as jam. Curd should be stored in the refrigerator.

Chutney is a sweet, spicy relish made with sugar and vinegar. It is cooked slowly to give a rich, full flavour. It may be very hot and spicy or mild and aromatic.

Relish is a cooked or pickled condiment, usually made with vegetables or fruit. It can be smooth or chunky and hot or mild.

Tapenade is a tasty spread that may include puréed or finely chopped olives, capers, anchovies and olive oil. It is a specialty of Provence, France.

Pesto traditionally contains crushed basil leaves, garlic, pine nuts, Parmesan and olive oil. It is an Italian sauce that is typically served with pasta. There are also other types of pesto you can make.

Pickles are vegetables preserved in a brine or vinegar mixture. They may be sour, sweet, hot or mild. Pickled vegetables stay crisp and have a tangy flavour.

The preserving process

Jams, marmalades and jellies are set, potted and sealed in a similar way. Vinegar-based preserves such as chutneys, relishes and pickles are treated a little differently, as are brine-based pickles. For all preserves, properly sterilised jars are essential (see page 7).

Jams and marmalades

Follow the individual recipe until the mixture reaches setting point. The setting point is the point when the fruit mixture is ready for potting. A good set depends on the amounts of pectin, acid (naturally found in fruit) and sugar in the mixture. Some jams reach setting point after just a few minutes boiling; others take 15 minutes or longer.

To tell when setting point has been reached:

- Remove the pan from the heat and put a little of the boiling mixture on a chilled saucer. (It is a good idea to have 3 or 4 saucers ready in the freezer or refrigerator.)

- As it cools, the jam will begin to set: it will wrinkle when pushed gently with a finger and will remain in two separate parts when a finger is drawn through it.

If using a sugar thermometer:

- Keep the thermometer in warm water until ready to use, so that the temperature of the boiling mixture isn't reduced too much when you put the thermometer in.

- To get an accurate reading, turn the thermometer around in the mixture and don't let it touch the base of the pan. Setting point is 110°C (220°F). If this hasn't been reached, return to the heat and boil for a few minutes only before testing again. Don't overcook; if the mixture is boiled for too long it won't set.

Potting and sealing

- Stand the warm to hot jars on a folded newspaper or wooden board to prevent cracking when the hot preserve is poured in.

- Pour the mixture into the jars. Fill them to the brim, as the jam will shrink a little as it cools. The less air space in the jars, the better the preserve will keep.

- If you forget to cover the jars while the jam is still hot, leave until completely cold; mould may grow on the surface if the jam is covered while warm.

- Wipe the outside of the filled jars and cover the surface of the jam with waxed circles, with the waxed side down. The whole of the disc should be in contact with the preserve, with no air bubbles underneath it.

- Seal tightly with metal screw-top lids or cellophane covers. If using cellophane covers:

  o Allow the preserve to cool before applying wetted cellophane covers. If these are applied before the jam is cooled, water can condense inside the covers, causing mould.

  o Moisten one side of the cellophane cover with a drop of water and place it, with the damp side facing upwards, on the jar. Secure the cellophane cover with an elastic band and leave to dry; as the cover dries, it will contract and form a tight seal.

- Label jars with the name of the jam and the date, and store in a cool, dark, dry and well-ventilated place. Most jams will keep for up to a year. Once opened, store in the refrigerator.

Jellies

Fruits with a high pectin content are best for jelly-making. The fruit should be cooked slowly to extract the pectin.

Straining and setting

- The jelly bag should be scalded by pouring boiling water through it, so the fruit juices don't soak into it.
- Suspend the jelly bag from a hook or from the legs of an upturned stool or chair and place a large bowl underneath.
- Ladle the fruit pulp and juices into the jelly bag and leave overnight. Don't squeeze the jelly bag to speed up the process or the jelly will be cloudy.
- As per individual recipes, the strained juice is boiled with sugar until setting point is reached. Cooking time can vary from 30 minutes to more than an hour.

Potting and sealing

Jellies are potted in the same manner as jams and marmalades.

- Jellies are best potted as soon as possible; if left to stand, they start to gel in the pan.
- Remove any foam from the top of the jelly with a metal spoon, or stir slowly to disperse. To avoid air bubbles forming, tilt the jar and pour in the hot jelly slowly.

- Because of the method used to extract the juice, it is difficult to estimate the final amount, so prepare more jars than you think you will need.
- Don't move the jars until the jelly has set completely.
- Once opened, store in the refrigerator.

Preserves in vinegar

Vinegar is a key ingredient in chutney, relishes and pickles, acting as a powerful preservative and contributing to flavour. When making preserves it is important to use good quality vinegar with an acid content of at least 5 per cent – never use anything labelled 'non-brewed condiment'. Different vinegars give different flavours.

- Hot chutney should be poured into warm sterilised jars right up to the brim and covered while still hot. Chutney will taste better if left to mature for at least 3 months and will keep in a cool, dry, dark place for 2 to 3 years. Once opened, store in the refrigerator.
- Sweet pickles are made by simmering fruit or vegetables with vinegar, sugar and spices. After potting, the vinegar syrup is boiled down until reduced then poured over the fruit in the jars. Shake the jars occasionally during storage to distribute the fruit and syrup evenly. When making sweet pickles, be careful not to overcook; the fruit should retain a firm texture.
- For chutneys and pickles, lids must be vinegar-proof – for example, lined with plastic. Plastic lids from coffee jars are perfect. If you only have metal lids, line them with a disc of waxed paper first. Lids must be airtight.

Preserves in brine

- Pickling salt or sea salt is best for brining; table salt has additives that tend to make the brine cloudy.
- Pickles must be stored in a cool, dark, dry place to prevent discolouration. They are best left for at least one month before using. Once opened, store in the refrigerator.

Kitchen essentials

Thanks to modern equipment, it is quicker and easier than ever to make tasty preserves.

- Use a large, deep **heavy-based pan** with plenty of room for the mixture to boil rapidly without boiling over. It is worth investing in a special preserving pan if you intend to make lots of preserves. For chutneys and pickles, use a stainless steel or aluminium pan; never brass, copper or iron. Vinegar will react with and corrode these metals.

- A sturdy **wooden spoon** with a long handle will keep your hands away from the boiling mixture.

- For jelly-making you will need a **jelly bag**, or a **jelly strainer**.

- For pickles, use a **nylon sieve**, as metal could adversely affect the colour and flavour of the finished pickles.

- **Glass jars** with rubber seals and metal lids are available in a range of sizes. The jars must be airtight. You can buy **special preserving packs** containing glass jars and metal lids.

- Packs of **waxed circles**, **transparent cellophane covers** and **elastic bands** are available from cookware and kitchen shops.

- A heat-resistant wide **funnel** is helpful when filling jars, but a **jug** or a small **ladle** can be used instead.

- A **sugar or preserving thermometer** is useful, but not essential

Note: Don't use the same utensils for making vinegar preserves and jam; cross-contamination will spoil the flavour of the jam.

Sterilising jars

Jars must be scrupulously clean and sterilised before being filled.

- Wash the jars in hot, soapy water, rinse well and put in a low oven for 15 to 20 minutes until warm and completely dry.

- Sterilise all lids in boiling water for 10 minutes. Keep the lids in the hot water until ready for use, then dry with kitchen paper.

- Depending on the recipe, jars may be filled when hot, warm or cold.

Jams &
Marmalades

I got the blues thinking of the future,
so I left off and made some marmalade.
It's amazing how it cheers one up to
shred oranges and scrub the floor.

D. H. Lawrence (1885–1930)

Orange Marmalade

Prep and cook time: 2 h 35 min
Standing: 20 min
Difficulty: medium
Makes: 4 kg | 141 oz marmalade

1500 g | 53 oz oranges
2 lemons, juice
3400 ml | 115 fl oz water
3000 g | 106 oz white
    (granulated) sugar, warmed
    in a very low oven

1   Cut the oranges in half and squeeze out the juice and pips.
    Cut away any thick white pith from the peel and finely shred
    the peel with a sharp knife.

2   Roughly chop the pith and tie loosely in a piece of muslin with
    the orange flesh and pips.

3   Put the shredded peel, orange and lemon juices, muslin bag
    and water into a large heavy-based pan. Place over a low heat
    and slowly bring to a boil.

4   Reduce the heat and simmer gently for 1½–2 hours, until the
    peel is tender. Remove the muslin bag, squeezing the juices
    into the pan.

5   Stir in the warmed sugar until completely dissolved and then
    bring to a boil. Boil rapidly for about 15 minutes until setting
    point is reached. Skim off any scum from the surface and leave
    to stand for 10–20 minutes.

6   Stir once. Pour into hot sterilised jars, cover, seal and label.

Kumquat Marmalade

Prep and cook time: 1 h 30 min
Difficulty: easy
Makes: 1–2 kg | 35–71 oz
  marmalade

675 g | 24 oz kumquats, sliced
900 ml | 32 fl oz | 4 cups water
900 g | 32 oz | 4 cups white
  (granulated) sugar
2 tbsp lemon juice

1 Put the kumquat slices in a
   pan and cover with the
   water. Cover and leave to
   stand overnight.

2 Heat the kumquats and
   water to simmering
   point and cook gently until
   tender.

3 Add the sugar and lemon
   juice and cook, stirring over
   a low heat until the sugar
   has dissolved. Increase the
   heat and boil rapidly until
   setting point is reached.
   Stand for 10 minutes.

4 Stir and spoon into hot
   sterilised jars, cover and seal.

Apple Blackberry Marmalade

Prep and cook time: 1 h
Difficulty: easy
Makes: 2–3 kg | 71–106 oz
  marmalade

675 g | 24 oz cooking apples, peeled
  and cored weight, chopped
150 ml | 5 fl oz | ⅔ cup water
1000 g | 35 oz blackberries
1400 g | 49 oz | 6 cups white
  (granulated) sugar

1 Put the apples into a large
   heavy-based pan with the
   water. Bring to a boil,
   then simmer gently for
   10 minutes.

2 Add the blackberries and
   continue to simmer gently
   for about 10 minutes until
   soft and pulpy.

3 Stir in the sugar until
   completely dissolved and
   then bring to a boil.

4 Boil rapidly for about
   15–20 minutes until setting
   point is reached.

5 Pour into hot sterilised jars,
   cover, seal and label.

Mango Jam

Prep and cook time: 30 min
Difficulty: easy
Makes: 750 g | 26 oz jam

450 g | 16 oz mango, peeled and
  pitted weight
2 tbsp water
2 tbsp lemon juice
450 g | 16 oz | 2 cups white
  (granulated) sugar

1 Put the mango flesh into a
   pan with the water and
   lemon juice. Bring to a
   simmer and simmer gently
   until the fruit is soft.

2 Add the sugar and stir over
   a low heat until the sugar
   has dissolved.

3 Bring to a boil and boil
   rapidly until setting point
   is reached.

4 Spoon into hot sterilised
   jars, cover, seal and label.

Raspberry Jam

Prep and cook time: 40 min
Difficulty: medium
Makes: 2 jars

500 g | 18 oz | 4 cups raspberries
350 g | 12 oz | 1½ cups caster
 (berry) sugar
1 tsp lemon juice

1 Heat the oven to 200°C
   (180°C fan | 400°F | gas 6).

2 Put the raspberries into a
   heatproof dish, do the same
   with the sugar and place
   both dishes in the oven for
   20–30 minutes. The berries
   should still have shape –
   check after 20 minutes.
   The fruit and sugar should
   be very hot.

3 Carefully combine the
   hot sugar and hot berries
   and lemon juice; stir
   together. The berries will
   dissolve with the sugar,
   creating instant jam. Ladle
   into sterilised jars and seal
   tightly.

Grandma's Note
This jam will keep in the refrigerator
for a few weeks only.

Blackberry Jam

Prep and cook time: 40 min
Difficulty: medium
Makes: 1.5 kg | 53 oz jam

900 g | 32 oz blackberries
900 g | 32 oz | 4 cups white
  (granulated) sugar
2 tbsp lemon juice

1 Put the berries into a large
   heavy-based pan and cook
   over a low heat until soft
   and pulpy. Press the fruit
   with a wooden spoon as it
   cooks, to extract the juices.

2 Add the sugar and lemon
   juice and stir over a
   low heat until the sugar
   has dissolved.

3 Increase the heat and boil
   rapidly until setting point
   is reached.

4 Spoon into hot sterilised
   jars and seal tightly.

Plum and Apple Jam

Prep and cook time: 35 min
Difficulty: easy
Makes: 2 kg | 71 oz jam

450 g | 16 oz cooking apples,
   peeled, cored and chopped
900 g | 32 oz plums, pitted and
   halved
4 tbsp water
1300 g | 46 oz | 6 cups white
   (granulated) sugar

1 Put the fruit and water into a large heavy-based pan. Heat gently to boiling point, then reduce the heat, cover the pan and simmer very gently until the fruit is soft – if it starts to stick to the pan add a little more water.

2 Stir in the sugar until completely dissolved, then bring to a boil. Boil rapidly until setting point is reached.

3 Spoon into hot sterilised jars, cover, seal and label.

Gooseberry Jam

Prep and cook time: 1 h 15 min
Difficulty: easy
Makes: 2–3 kg | 71–106 oz jam

675 g | 24 oz hard green
gooseberries, topped and tailed
675 g | 24 oz red gooseberries,
topped and tailed
600 ml | 21 fl oz | 2½ cups water
1500 g | 53 oz | 6 cups white
(granulated) sugar

1 Put the gooseberries and
water into a large heavy-
based pan. Heat gently to
boiling point, then reduce
the heat, cover the pan and
simmer very gently for
about 20–30 minutes until
the skins are soft, stirring
from time to time to
prevent the fruit sticking.
The actual time will depend
on the ripeness of the fruit.

2 Stir in the sugar until
completely dissolved and
then bring to a boil.

3 Boil rapidly for about
15–20 minutes until setting
point is reached.

4 Pour into warm sterilised
jars, cover, seal and label.

Redcurrant, Cherry and Pear Jam

Prep and cook time: 45 min
Difficulty: medium
Makes: 1 kg | 35 oz jam

250 g | 9 oz redcurrants
water
450 g | 16 oz cherries, pitted weight
2 pears, peeled, cored and chopped
400 g | 14 oz | 1¾ cups white
  (granulated) sugar
1 tbsp lemon juice

1 Put the redcurrants and a little water into a pan over a low heat. Simmer very gently until tender, crushing the berries to release their juices. Remove from the heat and push through a sieve into a bowl to remove the seeds.

2 Put the cherries and pears into a large heavy-based pan with a little water. Bring to a simmer and cook very gently until the fruit is tender. Add the redcurrant puree, sugar and lemon juice and boil steadily until setting point is reached. Remove from the heat and allow to cool slightly.

3 Stir once, then spoon into hot sterilised jars, cover, seal and label.

Fig and Lemon Jam

Prep and cook time: 45 min
Difficulty: easy
Makes: 750 g | 26 oz jam

450 g | 16 oz figs, halved
   or quartered
2 tbsp water
2 tbsp finely grated lemon zest
450 g | 16 oz | 2 cups white
   (granulated) sugar
2 tbsp lemon juice

1 Put the figs, water and
   lemon zest into a large pan.
   Bring to a boil, then reduce
   the heat and simmer until
   the figs are soft.

2 Add the sugar and lemon
   juice and stir over a low
   heat until the sugar has
   dissolved. Bring to a boil
   and boil rapidly until
   setting point is reached.

3 Remove from the heat and
   allow to cool slightly. Stir
   once and spoon into hot
   sterilised jars. Cover, seal
   and label.

Berry and Cherry Jam

Prep and cook time: 40 min
Difficulty: easy
Makes: 750–900 g | 26–32 oz jam

450 g | 16 oz mixed blueberries
   and cherries, pitted
1 cooking apple, peeled, cored
   and chopped
1 lemon, juice
white (granulated) sugar,
   see recipe

1 Put all the fruit into a pan with the lemon juice. Bring to a boil, then reduce the heat and simmer gently until the fruit is soft. Remove from the heat and allow to cool slightly.

2 Measure the pulp. For each 225 ml | 7½ fl oz | 1 cup, add 175 g | 6 oz | ¾ cup sugar.

3 Return to the pan and cook gently until the sugar has dissolved. Bring to a boil and boil rapidly until setting point is reached. Remove from the heat. and allow to cool slightly.

4 Stir once, then spoon into hot sterilised jars, cover, seal and label.

Apricot Jam

Prep and cook time: 1 h 10 min
Difficulty: easy
Makes: 3 kg | 106 oz jam

2000 g | 71 oz fresh apricots,
   halved
450 ml | 16 fl oz | 2 cups water
1 lemon, juice
2000 g | 71 oz | 8 cups white
   (granulated) sugar

1 Put the apricots into a large
   heavy-based pan with the
   water and bring to a boil.
   Reduce the heat and
   simmer gently for about
   20 minutes until soft.

2 Stir in the lemon juice and
   sugar until completely
   dissolved and then bring to
   a boil.

3 Boil rapidly for about
   15–20 minutes until setting
   point is reached.

4 Pour into warm sterilised
   jars, cover, seal and label.

Red Grape Jam

Prep and cook time: 30 min
Difficulty: easy
Makes: 750 g | 26 oz jam

450 g | 16 oz seedless red grapes
2 tbsp red wine
450 g | 16 oz | 2 cups white
   (granulated) sugar
2 tbsp lemon juice

1 Put the grapes and wine
   into a pan and bring to a
   simmer. Cook gently until
   the grapes are soft.

2 Add the sugar and lemon
   juice and stir over a low
   heat until the sugar has
   dissolved. Bring to a boil
   and boil rapidly until
   setting point is reached.

3 Spoon into hot sterilised
   jars, cover, seal and label.

Rose Hip Jam

Prep and cook time: 40 min
Cooling: 20 min
Difficulty: medium
Makes: 750 g | 26 oz jam

450 g | 16 oz rose hips, weight
   after seeds removed and
   chopped
250 ml | 9 fl oz | 1 cup water
white (granulated) sugar,
   see recipe

1 Put the rose hips and water into a pan and bring to a boil. Reduce
   the heat, cover and simmer gently until the rose hips are very soft.

2 Press the mixture through a sieve into a bowl and allow the
   pulp to cool.

3 Weigh the pulp and put into a pan with 100 g | 3½ oz | ½ cup
   sugar for every 100 g | 3½ oz pulp. Bring to a simmer and cook
   gently until the mixture thickens to a jam-like consistency.

4 Bring to a boil and boil rapidly, stirring, until setting point is
   reached. Skim the surface with a slotted spoon.

5 Spoon into hot sterilised jars, cover, seal and label.

Chilli Jam

Prep and cook time: 1 h 30 min
Difficulty: easy
Makes: 1 kg | 35 oz jam

8 red capsicums (peppers), seeds
   removed and chopped
8 red chillies, roughly chopped
5 cm | 2" piece root
   ginger (gingerroot), chopped
5 cloves garlic, finely chopped
400 g | 14 oz canned
   chopped tomatoes
750 g | 26 oz | 3⅓ cups white
   (granulated) sugar
250 ml | 9 fl oz | 1 cup red
wine vinegar

1 Put all the ingredients into a
   large pan and heat gently
   until the sugar has dissolved.

2 Bring to a boil and skim off
   any scum that rises to the
   surface. Reduce the heat
   and simmer gently for
   45–50 minutes until thick,
   stirring occasionally.

3 Continue cooking for a
   further 10–15 minutes,
   stirring frequently, until
   very thick. Remove from
   the heat and cool slightly.

4 Spoon into hot sterilised
   jars, cover, seal and label.

Blood Orange, Lime and Grapefruit Marmalades

Prep and cook time: 7 h
Difficulty: medium
Makes: 6 kg | 212 oz marmalade

For the blood orange marmalade:
450 g | 16 oz blood oranges
4 tbsp lemon juice
1800 ml | 61 fl oz | 7½ cups water
1500 g | 53 oz | 6 cups white
 (granulated) sugar, warmed in
 a very low oven.

For the grapefruit marmalade:
2 pink grapefruit
1500 ml | 51 fl oz | 6⅓ cups water
1100 g | 39 oz | 5 cups white
 (granulated) sugar, warmed in
 a very low oven.
4 tbsp lemon juice

For the lime marmalade:
450 g | 16 oz unwaxed limes
1500 ml | 51 fl oz | 6⅓ cups water
1100 g | 39 oz | 5 cups white
 (granulated) sugar, warmed in
 a very low oven
1½ tbsp lemon juice

For the blood orange marmalade:

1 Cut the oranges in half and squeeze out the juice and pips. Cut away any thick white pith from the peel and finely shred the peel with a sharp knife.

2 Roughly chop the pith and tie loosely in a piece of muslin with the orange flesh and pips.

3 Put the shredded peel, orange and lemon juices, muslin bag and water into a large heavy-based pan. Place over a low heat and slowly bring to a boil.

4 Reduce the heat and simmer gently for 1½–2 hours, until the peel is tender. Remove the muslin bag, squeezing the juices into the pan.

5 Stir in the warmed sugar until completely dissolved and then bring to a boil. Boil rapidly for about 15 minutes until setting point is reached. Skim off any scum from the surface and leave to stand for 10–20 minutes.

6 Stir once. Pour into hot sterilised jars, cover, seal and label.

For the grapefruit marmalade:

1 Cut the grapefruit in half and squeeze out the juice and pips. Cut away any thick white pith from the peel and finely shred the peel with a sharp knife.

2 Roughly chop the pith and tie loosely in a piece of muslin with the grapefruit flesh and pips.

3 Put the shredded peel, grapefruit and lemon juices, muslin bag and water into a large heavy-based pan. Place over a low heat and slowly bring to a boil.

4 Reduce the heat and simmer gently for 1½–2 hours, until the peel is tender. Remove the muslin bag, squeezing the juices into the pan.

5 Stir in the warmed sugar until completely dissolved and then bring to a boil. Boil rapidly for about 15 minutes until setting point is reached. Skim off

any scum from the surface and leave to stand for 10–20 minutes.

6 Stir once. Pour into hot sterilised jars, cover, seal and label.

For the lime marmalade:

1 Place the limes in boiling water for 3 minutes (this makes the fruit easier to peel).

2 Remove the rind from the limes with a vegetable peeler and cut into fine shreds. Remove the pith and chop the flesh.

3 Place the pith, flesh and pips in a muslin bag and put into the pan with the peel and water. Place over a low heat and slowly bring to a boil.

4 Reduce the heat and simmer gently for 1–1½ hours until the peel is tender. Remove the pan from the heat and squeeze the muslin bag into the mixture before discarding it.

5 Stir in the warm sugar and lemon juice and cook over a low heat, stirring all the time until completely dissolved. Bring to a boil and boil rapidly for about 10–15 minutes until setting point is reached.

6 Skim off any foam from the surface and leave to stand for 10 minutes.

7 Stir once. Pour into hot sterilised jars, cover, seal and label.

Carrot Jam

Prep and cook time: 35 min
Difficulty: easy
Makes: 750 g | 26 oz jam

450 g | 16 oz carrots, peeled
   weight, very thinly sliced
225 ml | 8 fl oz | 1 cup water
2 tsp finely grated lemon zest
450 g | 16 oz | 2 cups white
   (granulated) sugar
4 tbsp lemon juice
2 tbsp brandy

1 Put the carrots, water and
lemon zest into a pan and
bring to a boil. Cook
steadily until the carrots
are tender.

2 Add the sugar and cook,
stirring, over a low heat
until the sugar has
dissolved. Add the lemon
juice and brandy.

3 Bring to a boil and cook
rapidly until setting point
is reached.

4 Spoon into hot sterilised
jars, cover, seal and label.

Watermelon Jam

Prep and cook time: 50 min
Standing: 2 h
Difficulty: easy
Makes: 750 g | 26 oz jam

450 g | 16 oz watermelon flesh,
 cut into 2.5 cm | 1" dice
4 tbsp lemon juice
2 tbsp port
450 g | 16 oz | 2 cups white
 (granulated) sugar

1 Put the watermelon flesh,
 half the lemon juice, port
 and sugar into a pan and
 allow to stand for
 2 hours.

2 Heat gently, stirring, until
 the sugar has dissolved,
 then add the remaining
 lemon juice and increase
 the heat.

3 Cook steadily for
 20–30 minutes, until
 setting point is reached.
 Allow to stand for
 10 minutes.

4 Stir once, then spoon into
 hot sterilised jars. Cover,
 seal and label.

Strawberry Jam

Prep and cook time: 55 min
Standing: 15 min
Difficulty: easy
Makes: 2 kg | 71 oz jam

2000 g | 71 oz strawberries
1600 g | 56 oz | 7 cups white
   (granulated) sugar
8 tbsp lemon juice

1 Cut any very large
   strawberries into smaller
   pieces to speed up the
   cooking time.

2 Put the strawberries into a
   large heavy-based pan over
   a low heat and slowly bring
   to a boil.

3 Reduce the heat and
   simmer gently for about
   10–15 minutes until the
   fruit has softened.

4 Add the sugar and lemon
   juice and stir over a low
   heat until the sugar has
   dissolved completely.

5 Bring to a boil and
   boil rapidly for about
   15–20 minutes until setting
   point is reached. Skim off
   any foam and allow the jam
   to stand for 15 minutes, to
   ensure the strawberries are
   distributed evenly.

6 Pour into warm sterilised
   jars, cover, seal and label.

Quince Jam with Elderflower Syrup

Prep and cook time: 45 min
Standing: 10 min
Difficulty: easy
Makes: 750 g | 26 oz jam

500 g | 18 oz ripe quinces, peeled
   and cored weight, chopped
150 ml | 5 fl oz | ⅔ cup water
450 g | 16 oz | 2 cups white
   (granulated) sugar
1 tbsp lemon juice
3 tbsp elderflower cordial (liqueur)

1 Put the quinces and water
   into a large heavy-based
   pan. Bring to a simmer and
   simmer gently until the
   fruit is soft.

2 Add the sugar and lemon
   juice and stir over a low
   heat until the sugar
   has dissolved.

3 Bring to a boil and boil
   rapidly until setting point
   is reached. Stir in the
   elderflower cordial (liqueur)
   and leave to stand for
   10 minutes.

4 Stir and spoon into hot
   sterilised jars, cover, seal
   and label.

Apricot and Chilli Jam

Prep and cook time: 50 min
Difficulty: easy
Makes: 2 kg | 71 oz jam

450 g | 16 oz ready-to-eat
 dried apricots
1–2 red chillies, thinly sliced
1700 ml | 57½ fl oz | 7 cups water
1300 g | 46 oz | 6 cups white
 (granulated) sugar
4 tbsp lemon juice

1 Put the apricots, chillies and
 water into a large pan and
 bring to a boil. Reduce the
 heat and cook gently until
 the apricots and chillies are
 tender. Remove the chillies
 and set aside.

2 Add the sugar and lemon
 juice to the pan and stir
 over a low heat until the
 sugar has dissolved.

3 Bring to a boil and add the
 reserved chillies. Boil
 rapidly until setting point is
 reached. Remove from the
 heat and allow to cool until
 slightly thickened.

4 Stir once and spoon into
 hot sterlilised jars. Cover,
 seal and label.

Grandma's Note
For a milder flavour, remove
and discard the seeds from
the chillies.

Nectarine and Pineapple Jam

Prep and cook time: 1 h
Soaking: 4 h
Difficulty: easy
Makes: 2 kg | 71 oz jam

500 g | 18 oz ready-to-eat dried
   nectarines or peaches
1400 ml | 49 fl oz | 6 cups water
225 g | 8 oz canned
   crushed pineapple
1300 g | 46 oz | 6 cups jam
   sugar (see note)
4 tbsp lemon juice

1 Soak the nectarines in the
   water for 3–4 hours in a
   large heavy-based pan.

2 Cover the pan and bring to
   a simmer. Cook gently until
   the nectarines are tender.
   Remove the nectarines from
   the pan with a slotted spoon
   and cut into small dice.

3 Return the nectarines to the
   liquid in the pan with the
   pineapple, sugar and lemon
   juice and stir over a low heat
   until the sugar has dissolved.

4 Bring to a boil and boil
   rapidly until setting point is
   reached. Remove from the
   heat and allow to cool until
   slightly thickened.

5 Stir once and spoon into
   hot sterilised jars. Cover,
   seal and label.

Grandma's Note
Jam sugar has added pectin.

Pear and Chocolate Jam

Prep and cook time: 40 min
Difficulty: easy
Makes: 1–2 kg | 35–71 oz jam

1000 g | 35 oz pears, peeled,
   cored and chopped
1 lemon, juice
400 g | 14 oz | 2¾ cups white
   (granulated) sugar
150 g | 5 oz dark (semi-sweet)
   chocolate, 70% cocoa solids,
   broken

1 Mix together the pears and
   lemon juice. Put into a large
   pan with the sugar.

2 Heat gently until the sugar
   has dissolved, then simmer
   until the fruit is soft,
   stirring occasionally.

3 Stir in the chocolate and
   simmer very gently, stirring,
   until the chocolate has
   melted and is well blended.

4 Spoon into hot sterilised
   jars, cover, seal and label.
   Store in the refrigerator.

Strawberry and Passionfruit Jam

Prep and cook time: 25 min
Difficulty: easy
Makes: 500 g | 18 oz jam

400 g | 14 oz strawberries,
   quartered
6 passionfruit, pulp and seeds
1 lemon, juice
300 g | 11 oz | 2½ cups jam
   sugar, see note

1 Put the fruit into a pan with
   the lemon juice and sugar.
   Heat gently, stirring, until
   the sugar has dissolved.

2 Simmer for about 5 minutes
   until the strawberries are
   soft. Bring to a boil and
   boil rapidly until setting
   point is reached.

3 Spoon into hot sterilised
   jars, cover, seal and label.

Grandma's Note
Jam sugar has added pectin.

Blackcurrant Jam

Prep and cook time: 1 h
Difficulty: easy
Makes: 1 kg | 35 oz jam

450 g | 16 oz blackcurrants
300–450 ml | 11–16 fl oz |
   1⅓–2 cups water
550 g | 19 oz | 2½ cups white
   (granulated) sugar

1 Put the blackcurrants into a
   large heavy-based pan with
   the water (use the smaller
   amount of water if the fruit
   is very ripe) and slowly
   bring to the boil.

2 Reduce the heat and
   simmer gently for about
   20–30 minutes until the
   fruit is soft.

3 Add the sugar and stir over
   a low heat until the sugar
   has dissolved completely.

4 Bring to a boil and
   boil rapidly for about
   10–15 minutes until setting
   point is reached.

5 Spoon into hot sterilised
   jars, cover, seal and label.

Orange, Almond and Apricot Jam

Prep and cook time: 2 h
Difficulty: medium
Makes: 4 kg | 141 oz jam

900 g | 32 oz oranges
2 lemons
450 g | 16 oz ready-to-eat dried
   apricots, sliced
3500 ml | 118 fl oz | 15 cups water
3000 g | 106 oz | 12 cups white
   (granulated) sugar, warmed in
   a very low oven
25 g | 1 oz | ⅓ cup flaked almonds

1 Cut the oranges and lemons
   in half and squeeze out the
   juice and pips. Roughly
   chop the peel and pith and
   tie loosely in a piece of
   muslin with the orange and
   lemon flesh and pips.

2 Put the orange and lemon
   juices, apricots, muslin bag
   and water into a large
   heavy-based pan. Place over
   a low heat and slowly bring
   to a boil.

3 Reduce the heat and simmer
   gently for 1–1½ hours, until
   the fruit is tender. Remove
   the muslin bag, squeezing
   the juices into the pan.

4 Stir in the warmed sugar
   until completely dissolved
   and then bring to a boil.
   Boil rapidly for about
   15 minutes until setting
   point is reached. Skim off
   any scum from the surface
   and stir in the almonds.

5 Spoon into hot sterilised
   jars, cover, seal and label.

Cranberry Jam

Prep and cook time: 40 min
Difficulty: easy
Makes: 1 kg | 35 oz jam

450 g | 16 oz | 4 cups cranberries
150 ml | 5 fl oz | ⅔ cup water
550 g | 19 oz | 2½ cups white
  (granulated) sugar

1 Put the cranberries and
   water into a large heavy-
   based pan. Cover tightly
   and bring to a boil.

2 Reduce the heat and
   simmer very gently for
   10 minutes until the berries
   have softened.

3 Add the sugar and stir over
   a low heat until the sugar
   has dissolved.

4 Bring to a boil and boil
   rapidly until setting point
   is reached.

5 Spoon into hot sterilised
   jars, cover, seal and label.

Plum and Walnut Jam

Prep and cook time: 40 min
Difficulty: easy
Makes: 800 g | 28 oz jam

450 g | 16 oz hard red plums,
  pitted weight, halved
4 tbsp water
4 tbsp chopped ready-to-eat
  dried prunes
350 g | 12 oz | 1½ cups white
  (granulated) sugar
110 g | 4 oz | ½ cup brown sugar
75 g | 2½ oz | ¾ cup
  halved walnuts

1 Put the plums and water
   into a large heavy-based
   pan. Bring to a boil, then
   reduce the heat and simmer
   gently until soft and pulpy.
   Stir in the prunes.

2 Add both sugars and stir
   over a low heat until
   dissolved. Increase the heat
   and bring to a boil.

3 Stir in the walnuts and boil
   rapidly until setting point
   is reached.

4 Spoon into hot sterilised
   jars, cover, seal and label.

Jellies & Curds

It is probable that the lemon is the most valuable
of all fruit for preserving health.

Maud Grieve, A Modern Herbal *(1931)*

Apple Jelly with Chilli and Star Anise

Prep and cook time: 1 h 25 min
Straining: 12 h
Difficulty: medium
Makes: 700–850 g | 25–30 oz
  jelly

600 g | 21 oz cooking apples,
  unpeeled and chopped
1000 ml | 35 fl oz | 4 cups water
white (granulated) sugar,
  see recipe
1 tbsp lemon juice
dried red chillies
star anise

1 Put the chopped apples and cores into a large heavy-based pan with the water.

2 Bring to a boil, then reduce the heat and simmer until the apples soften and become pulpy, stirring occasionally.

3 Ladle the fruit and juices into a scalded jelly bag.

4 Strain through the jelly bag overnight into a bowl.

5 Measure the juice into a large heavy-based pan and to every 600 ml (21 fl oz) juice allow 450 g (16 oz) sugar.

6 Heat the juice and sugar with the lemon juice and stir over a low heat until the sugar has dissolved completely.

7 Bring to a boil and boil rapidly for about 10–20 minutes until setting point is reached.

8 Pour into hot sterilised jars, and add a dried chilli and a star anise to each jar. Cover, seal and label.

Lemon Curd

Prep and cook time: 40 min
Difficulty: easy
Makes: 450 g | 16 oz
*   lemon curd*

2 large unwaxed lemons, finely
   grated zest and juice
225 g | 8 oz | 1 cup caster
   (berry) sugar
110 g | 4 oz | ½ cup unsalted
   butter, diced
2 large eggs, lightly beaten

1 Put the lemon zest, juice,
   sugar and butter in a large
   heatproof bowl.

2 Place over a pan of
   simmering (not boiling)
   water and stir to dissolve
   the sugar.

3 Stir in the eggs and
   continue stirring for about
   20 minutes, until the
   mixture thickens enough to
   coat the back of a wooden
   spoon. Do not cook for too
   long, as the mixture will
   thicken more as it cools.

4 Pour into warm sterilised
   jars, cover with waxed discs
   and leave until cold before
   sealing tightly with
   cellophane covers or lids.
   Store in a cool place and use
   within 1 month.

Raspberry Jelly

Prep and cook time: 35 min
Straining: 12 h
Difficulty: medium
Makes: 1 kg | 35 oz jelly

900 g | 32 oz | 7¼ cups raspberries
150 ml | 5 fl oz | ⅔ cup water
white (granulated) sugar, see recipe
lemon juice, see recipe

1 Put the raspberries and water into a large heavy-based pan. Bring to a simmer and simmer gently until soft, crushing them to release their juice.

2 Ladle the fruit and juices into a scalded jelly bag. Strain the juice through the jelly bag overnight into a bowl. Do not squeeze the bag or the jelly will be cloudy.

3 Measure the juice into a large heavy-based pan and to every 600 ml | 21 fl oz juice allow 450 g | 16 oz sugar and 1 tablespoon lemon juice.

4 Heat the juice and sugar in the pan and stir over a low heat until the sugar has dissolved completely. Bring to a boil and boil rapidly until setting point is reached. Skim off any scum on the surface.

5 Pour into warm sterilised jars. Cover, seal and label.

Pear Jelly

Prep and cook time: 45 min
Straining: 12 h
Difficulty: medium
Makes: 800 g | 28 oz jelly

900 g | 32 oz pears, with peel and
cores, chopped
600 ml | 21 fl oz | 2½ cups water
jam sugar, see recipe

1 Put the pears into a large
heavy-based pan with the
water. Bring to a boil, then
reduce the heat and simmer
until soft. Crush well to
release their juices.

2 Ladle the fruit and juices into
a scalded jelly bag. Strain the
juice through the jelly bag
overnight into a bowl. Do
not squeeze the bag or the
jelly will be cloudy.

3 Measure the juice into a
large heavy-based pan and to
every 600 ml | 21 fl oz juice
allow 450 g | 16 oz sugar.

4 Heat the juice and sugar in
the pan and stir over a low
heat until the sugar has
dissolved completely. Bring
to a boil and boil rapidly
until setting point is reached.

5 Skim off any scum and
pour into hot sterilised jars.
Cover, seal and label.

Grandma's Note
Jam sugar has added pectin.

Redcurrant and Apple Jelly

Prep and cook time: 45 min
Difficulty: medium
Makes: 900 g | 32 oz jelly

900 g | 32 oz cooking apples,
   with peel and cores, chopped
450 g | 16 oz redcurrants
600 ml | 21 fl oz | 2½ cups water
white (granulated) sugar, see recipe

1 Put the apples and
    redcurrants into a large
    heavy-based pan with the
    water. Bring to a boil, then
    reduce the heat and simmer
    until soft. Crush the fruit
    well to release the juices.

2 Ladle the fruit and juices into
    a scalded jelly bag. Strain the
    juice through the jelly bag
    overnight into a bowl. Do
    not squeeze the bag or the
    jelly will be cloudy.

3 Measure the juice into a
    large heavy-based pan and to
    every 600 ml | 21 fl oz juice
    allow 450 g | 16 oz sugar.

4 Heat the juice and sugar in
    the pan and stir over a low
    heat until the sugar has
    dissolved completely. Bring
    to a boil and boil rapidly
    until setting point is reached.

5 Skim off any scum and
    pour into hot sterilised jars.
    Cover, seal and label.

Spiced Apple Jelly

Prep and cook time: 45 min
Straining: 12 h
Difficulty: medium
Makes: 800 g | 28 oz jelly

900 g | 32 oz cooking apples,
  with peel and cores, chopped
600 ml | 21 fl oz | 2½ cups water
2 cinnamon sticks, broken
2 cloves
2 star anise
white (granulated) sugar,
  see recipe

1 Put the apples into a large
   heavy-based pan with the
   water and spices. Bring to
   a boil, then reduce the
   heat and simmer until
   soft. Crush the apples
   well to release their
   juices. Discard or put
   aside the spices. See note.

2 Ladle the fruit and juices
   into a scalded jelly bag.
   Strain the juice through
   the jelly bag overnight
   into a bowl. Do not
   squeeze the bag or the
   jelly will be cloudy.

3 Measure the juice into a
   large heavy-based pan and to
   every 600 ml | 21 fl oz juice
   allow 450 g | 16 oz sugar.

4 Heat the juice and sugar in
   the pan and stir over a low
   heat until the sugar has
   dissolved completely. Bring
   to a boil and boil rapidly
   until setting point is reached.

5 Skim off any scum and
   pour into warm sterilised
   jars. Cover, seal and label.

Grandma's Note
You can add the spices to the
filled jars, just before sealing.

Ginger Jelly

Prep and cook time: 50 min
Straining: 12 h
Difficulty: medium
Makes: 800 g | 28 oz jelly

900 g | 32 oz cooking apples,
  with peel and cores, chopped
600 ml | 21 fl oz | 2½ cups water
25 g | 1 oz root ginger
  (gingerroot), bruised
white (granulated) sugar,
  see recipe
5 cm | 2" piece root ginger
  (gingerroot), thinly sliced

1 Put the apples into a large
   heavy-based pan with the
   water and bruised ginger
   (gingerroot). Bring to a
   boil, then reduce the heat
   and simmer until soft.
   Crush the apples well to
   release their juices. Discard
   the ginger.

2 Ladle the fruit and juices
   into a scalded jelly bag.
   Strain the juice through
   the jelly bag overnight into
   a bowl. Do not squeeze
   the bag or the jelly will
   be cloudy.

3 Measure the juice into
   a large heavy-based
   pan and to every
   600 ml | 21 fl oz juice
   allow 450 g | 16 oz sugar.

4 Heat the juice and sugar in
   the pan. Add the sliced
   ginger and stir over a low
   heat until the sugar has
   dissolved completely. Bring
   to a boil and boil rapidly
   until setting point is reached.

5 Skim off any scum and
   stand for 10 minutes.

6 Stir once and pour into
   warm sterilised jars. Cover,
   seal and label.

Orange and Lemon Jelly

Prep and cook time: 2 h 20 min
Soaking: 12 h
Difficulty: medium
Makes: 1 kg | 35 oz jelly

450 g | 16 oz oranges
1800 ml | 61 fl oz | 8 cups water
1300 g | 46 oz | 6 cups white
  (granulated) sugar
4 tbsp lemon juice
2 tbsp thyme leaves

1 Cut the oranges in half and
  squeeze out the juice. Set
  aside in the refrigerator.

2 Chop the peel (with the
  pith). Remove the pips. Put
  the peel and pips into a pan
  with the water. Cover and
  soak overnight.

3 Heat the water, peel and
  pips and bring to a boil.
  Reduce the heat and
  simmer gently for 1½ hours.

4 Strain the liquid into a large
  heavy-based pan. Discard
  the peel and pips.

5 Add the sugar, orange and
  lemon juices and thyme to
  the pan and stir over a low
  heat until the sugar has
  dissolved. Bring to a boil
  and boil rapidly until
  setting point is reached.

6 Pour into hot sterilised jars,
  cover, seal and label.

Crabapple Jelly

Prep and cook time: 2 h 10 min
Straining: 12 h
Difficulty: medium
Makes: 1–2 kg | 35–71 oz jelly

2000 g | 71 oz crabapples, cut
   into quarters
1500 ml | 51 fl oz | 6¼ cups water
3–4 cloves (optional)
white (granulated) sugar,
   see recipe

1 Put the crabapples (there's
no need to peel or core
them) into a large heavy-
based pan with the water
and cloves if using.

2 Place over a low heat and
slowly bring to a boil.
Reduce the heat and
simmer gently for about
1½ hours until the fruit is
soft and pulpy.

3 Ladle the fruit and juices
into a scalded jelly bag.
Strain the juice through
the jelly bag overnight
into a bowl. Do not
squeeze the bag or the jelly
will be cloudy.

4 Measure the juice into a
large heavy-based pan
and to every 600 ml |
21 fl oz juice allow
450 g | 16 oz sugar.

5 Heat the juice and sugar in
the pan and stir over a low
heat until the sugar has
dissolved completely. Bring
to a boil and boil rapidly for
about 10–20 minutes until
setting point is reached.

6 Pour into warm sterilised
jars, cover, seal and label.

Apple and Cranberry Jelly

Prep and cook time: 45 min
Difficulty: medium
Makes: 1 kg | 35 oz jelly

900 g | 32 oz cooking apples,
   chopped with peel and cores
450 g | 16 oz | 4 cups cranberries
825 ml | 29 fl oz | 3½ cups water
white (granulated)sugar,
   see recipe

1 Put the apples and cranberries into a large pan with the water. Cover the pan tightly and bring to a boil.

2 Reduce the heat and simmer gently until the fruit is soft. Crush the fruit with a wooden spooon to release the juices.

3 Ladle the fruit and juices into a scalded jelly bag. Strain the juice through the jelly bag overnight into a bowl. Do not squeeze the bag or the jelly will be cloudy.

4 Measure the juice into a large heavy-based pan and to every 600 mL | 21 fl oz juice allow 450 g | 16 oz sugar.

5 Heat the juice and sugar in the pan and stir over a low heat until the sugar has dissolved completely. Bring to a boil and boil rapidly until setting point is reached.

6 Pour into hot sterilised jars. Cover, seal and label.

Chilli Jelly

Prep and cook time: 1 h 30 min
Straining: 12 h
Standing: 15 min
Difficulty: medium
Makes: 1 kg | 35 oz jelly

1300 g | 46 oz tomatoes, halved
3 unwaxed lemons, roughly
   chopped with peel
3 red chillies, seeds removed,
   1 roughly chopped, 2 thinly sliced
450 ml | 16 fl oz | 2 cups water
2 green chillies, seeds removed
650 g | 23 oz | 2¾ cups jam
   sugar, see note

1 Put the tomatoes, lemons,
chopped red chillies and
water in a large pan. Bring
to a boil, then reduce the
heat, cover and simmer very
gently for 40 minutes.

2 Ladle the pulp and juices
into a scalded jelly bag.
Strain the juice through
the jelly bag overnight
into a bowl. Do not
squeeze the bag or the jelly
will be cloudy.

3 Measure the juice into a
large heavy-based pan
and to every 500 ml |
17 fl oz juice allow
325 g | 11 oz sugar.

4 Heat the juice and sugar in
the pan and stir over a low
heat until the sugar has
dissolved completely. Bring
to a boil and stir in the sliced
red chillies and green chillies.
Boil rapidly until setting
point is reached. Skim off
any scum and leave to stand
for 15 minutes.

5 Pour into hot sterilised jars.
Cover, seal and label.

Grandma's Note
Jam sugar has added pectin.

Rose Jelly

Prep and cook time: 15 min
Standing: 20 min
Difficulty: easy
Makes: 750 g | 26 oz jelly

110 g | 4 oz rose petals, see note
250 ml | 9 fl oz | 1 cup
   boiling water
500 g | 18 oz | 2¼ cups caster
   (berry) sugar
1 lemon, juice
190 ml | 7 fl oz | ¾ cup
   liquid pectin
few drops rosewater

1 Put the rose petals into a
  bowl and pour over the
  boiling water to cover.
  Cover and leave to stand for
  20 minutes.

2 Strain the liquid through a
  sieve into a measuring jug.
  Make up to 250 ml if
  necessary with boiling water.

3 Pour into a pan and stir
  in the sugar and lemon
  juice until the sugar
  has dissolved.

4 Remove from the heat and
  stir in the pectin. Bring
  to a boil and boil rapidly
  for 1 minute. Stir in the
  rosewater.

5 Pour into hot sterilised jars.
  Cover, seal and label.

Grandma's Note

Use heavily scented red or pink petals that
are free from chemicals and pesticides —
roses bought from a florist aren't suitable.
Remove the heel — the white part at the
base (this has a bitter flavour) — and
wash the flowers gently before use.

Orange Curd

Prep and cook time: 40 min
Difficulty: easy
Makes: 450 g | 16 oz curd

3 large unwaxed oranges, finely
  grated zest and juice
1 tbsp lemon juice
225 g | 8 oz | 1 cup caster (berry)
  sugar
110 g | 4 oz | ½ cup unsalted
  butter, diced
2 large eggs, lightly beaten

1   Put the orange zest, juice,
    lemon juice, sugar and butter
    in a large heatproof bowl.

2   Place over a pan of
    simmering (not boiling)
    water and stir to dissolve
    the sugar.

3   Stir in the eggs and
    continue stirring for about
    20 minutes, until the
    mixture thickens enough to
    coat the back of a wooden
    spoon. Do not cook for too
    long, as the mixture will
    thicken more as it cools.

4   Pour into warmed sterilised
    jars, cover with waxed discs
    and leave until cold before
    sealing tightly with
    cellophane covers or lids.
    Store in a cool place and use
    within 1 month.

Elderflower Jelly

Prep and cook time: 2 h 20 min
Soaking: 12 h
Difficulty: medium
Makes: 1 kg | 35 oz jelly

450 g | 16 oz unwaxed lemons
1800 ml | 61 fl oz | 8 cups water
4 heads elderflowers
1300 g | 46 oz | 6 cups white
   (granulated) sugar
4 tbsp lemon juice

1 Coarsely grate the rind
   from 2 lemons. Cut the
   lemons in half and squeeze
   out the juice. Set the juice
   aside in the refrigerator.

2 Chop the peel (with the
   pith). Remove the pips.
   Put the peel and pips into
   a muslin bag and put into
   a large pan. Add the grated
   rind to the pan with
   the water. Cover and
   soak overnight.

3 Heat the water, peel, pips,
   grated rind and 2 heads
   elderflowers and bring to a
   boil. Reduce the heat
   and simmer gently for
   1½ hours.

4 Strain the liquid into a large
   heavy-based pan. Discard
   the muslin bag of peel and
   pips and the elderflowers.

5 Add the sugar, the reserved
   lemon juice and the
   4 tablespoons of lemon
   juice and the remaining
   elderflower heads to the pan
   and stir over a low heat
   until the sugar has
   dissolved. Bring to a boil
   and boil rapidly until
   setting point is reached. You
   can discard the elderflowers
   if you wish or keep them in
   the jelly.

6 Pour into hot sterilised jars,
   cover, seal and label.

Orange Jelly

Prep and cook time: 35 min
Difficulty: medium
Makes: 3 kg | 106 oz jelly

6 oranges
1 lemon, juice
450 ml | 16 fl oz | 2 cups water
1100 g | 39 oz | 5¼ cups white
   (granulated) sugar
250 ml | 9 fl oz | 1 cup
   liquid pectin

1 Squeeze the juice from 4 oranges and put into a measuring jug with the lemon juice. If it is less than 450 ml | 16 fl oz | 2 cups, squeeze the juice from one of the remaining oranges and make up to the required amount. Thinly slice the remaining orange or oranges.

2 Put the orange peel from the squeezed oranges into a pan with the water and bring to a boil. Cover and simmer for 10 minutes. Remove the orange peel and pour the liquid into a measuring jug. If it is more than 150 ml | 5 fl oz | ⅔ cup, return to the pan and boil rapidly until reduced to this amount.

3 Return the liquid to the pan and add the sugar and orange slices. Stir over a low heat until the sugar has dissolved, then increase the heat and boil rapidly for 2 minutes. Remove from the heat and stir in the pectin.

4 Bring to a boil and boil for 30 seconds. Skim off any scum.

5 Pour into hot sterilised jars, cover, seal and label.

Strawberry Jelly with Green Pepper

Prep and cook time: 40 min
Straining: 12 h
Difficulty: medium
Makes: 800 g | 28 oz jelly

900 g | 32 oz strawberries
1–2 tbsp green peppercorns
white (granulated) sugar, see recipe
lemon juice, see recipe

1 Put the strawberries and 2 teaspoons of the peppercorns into a large heavy-based pan. Bring to a boil, then reduce the heat and simmer until soft. Crush well to release their juices.

2 Ladle the fruit and juices into a scalded jelly bag. Strain the juice through the jelly bag overnight into a bowl. Do not squeeze the bag or the jelly will be cloudy.

3 Measure the juice into a large heavy-based pan and to every 600 ml | 21 fl oz juice allow 400 g | 14 oz sugar and 3 tablespoons lemon juice.

4 Heat the juice, sugar and lemon juice in the pan and stir over a low heat until the sugar has dissolved completely. Add the remaining peppercorns, bring to a boil and boil rapidly until setting point is reached.

5 Skim off any scum and pour into hot sterilised jars. Cover, seal and label.

Pomegranate Jelly

Prep and cook time: 20 min
Difficulty: easy
Makes: 1 kg | 35 oz jelly

1000 ml | 35 fl oz | 4 cups
   pomegranate juice
1500 g | 53 oz | 6 cups white
   (granulated) sugar
2 lemons, juice
175 ml | 6 fl oz | ¾ cup
   liquid pectin

1 Put the pomegranate juice, sugar and lemon juice into a large pan.

2 Heat gently until the sugar has dissolved completely, then increase the heat and bring to a boil.

3 Remove from the heat and stir in the pectin. Bring to a boil, and boil for 30 seconds. Remove from the heat and skim off any scum.

4 Pour into hot, sterilised jars. Cover, seal and label.

Quince Jelly

Prep and cook time: 1 h 30 min
Straining: 12 h
Difficulty: medium
Makes: 1 kg | 35 oz jelly

1000 g | 35 oz hard under-ripe
   quinces, scrubbed
900–1500 ml | 32–53 fl oz |
   4–6 cups water
white (granulated) sugar, see recipe

1 Cut the quinces into rough pieces (there's no need to peel or core them) and put into a large heavy-based pan with the water.

2 Place over a low heat and slowly bring to a boil. Reduce the heat and simmer gently for about 40–50 minutes until the fruit is reduced to a pulp.

3 Ladle the fruit and juices into a scalded jelly bag. Strain through the jelly bag overnight into a large bowl.

4 Measure the juice into a large heavy-based pan and to every 600 ml | 21 fl oz juice allow 450 g | 16 oz sugar.

5 Heat the juice and sugar and stir over a low heat until the sugar has dissolved completely.

6 Bring to a boil and boil rapidly for about 15 minutes until setting point is reached.

7 Pour into warm sterilised jars, cover, seal and label.

Rhubarb and Grape Jelly

Prep and cook time: 40 min
Straining: 12 h
Difficulty: medium
Makes: 1 kg | 35 oz jelly

900 g | 32 oz rhubarb, cut
   into chunks
450 g | 16 oz grapes
2 tbsp water
white (granulated) sugar,
   see recipe
lemon juice, see recipe

1 Put the rhubarb and grapes
   into a pan with the water.
   Bring to a boil, then reduce
   the heat and simmer until
   soft. Crush well to release
   their juices.

2 Ladle the fruit and juices into
   a scalded jelly bag. Strain the
   juice through the jelly bag
   overnight into a bowl. Do
   not squeeze the bag or the
   jelly will be cloudy.

3 Measure the juice into a
   large heavy-based pan and to
   every 600 ml | 21 fl oz juice
   allow 450 g | 16 oz sugar
   and 2 tablespoons lemon
   juice.

4 Heat the juice and sugar in
   the pan and stir over a low
   heat until the sugar has
   dissolved completely.
   Bring to a boil and boil
   rapidly until setting point is
   reached.

5 Skim off any scum and
   pour into hot sterilised jars.
   Cover, seal and label.

Cranberry Curd

Prep and cook time: 45 min
Difficulty: medium
Makes: 650 g | 23 oz curd

225 g | 8 oz | 2 cups cranberries
2 tbsp water
180 g | 6 oz | ¾ cup
  unsalted butter
270 g | 10 oz | 1¼ cups caster
  (berry) sugar
6 eggs, beaten

1 Place the cranberries and water in a pan and bring to a boil. Cover, reduce the heat and simmer gently for 5 minutes.

2 Press through a sieve into a large heatproof bowl. Stir in the butter and sugar.

3 Place the bowl over a pan of simmering (not boiling) water and stir to dissolve the sugar.

4 Stir in the eggs and continue stirring for about 20 minutes, until the mixture thickens enough to coat the back of a wooden spoon. Do not cook for too long, as the mixture will thicken more as it cools.

5 Pour into warm sterilised jars, cover with waxed discs and leave until cold before sealing tightly with cellophane covers or lids. Store in a cool place and use within 1 month.

Lime Curd

Prep and cook time: 40 min
Difficulty: easy
Makes: 450 g | 16 oz curd

3 unwaxed limes, juice
225 g | 8 oz | 1 cup caster
  (berry) sugar
150 g | 5 oz | ⅔ cup
  unsalted butter
2 large eggs, lightly beaten
2 egg yolks, lightly beaten

1 Put the lime juice, sugar
   and butter in a large
   heatproof bowl.

2 Place over a pan of simmering
   (not boiling) water and stir to
   dissolve the sugar.

3 Stir in the eggs and yolks
   and continue stirring for
   about 20 minutes, until the
   mixture thickens enough to
   coat the back of a wooden
   spoon. Do not cook for too
   long, as the mixture will
   thicken more as it cools.

4 Pour into warm sterilised
   jars, cover with waxed discs
   and leave until cold before
   sealing tightly with
   cellophane covers or lids.
   Store in a cool place and use
   within 1 month.

Elderberry Jelly

Prep and cook time: 1 h 10 min
Straining: 12 h
Difficulty: medium
Makes: 800 g | 28 oz jelly

1800 g | 63 oz elderberries
140 ml | 5 fl oz | ⅝ cup water
2 lemons, juice
white (granulated) sugar,
  see recipe

1 Put the elderberries into a
   large heavy-based pan.
   Crush well to release their
   juice, then add the water.
   Bring to a boil, cover
   and simmer for about
   15 minutes or until tender.

2 Ladle the fruit and juices into
   a scalded jelly bag. Strain the
   juice through the jelly bag
   overnight into a bowl.
   Do not squeeze the bag or
   the jelly will be cloudy.

3 Measure the juice into a
   large heavy-based pan and to
   every 600 ml | 21 fl oz juice
   allow 450 g | 16 oz sugar.
   Stir in the lemon juice.

4 Heat the juice and sugar in
   the pan and stir over a low
   heat until the sugar has
   dissolved completely. Bring
   to a boil and boil rapidly
   until setting point is reached.

5 Skim off any scum
   and pour into warm
   sterilised jars. Cover, seal
   and label.

Gooseberry and Rose Petal Jelly

Prep and cook time: 45 min
Straining: 12 h
Difficulty: medium
Makes: 750 g | 26 oz jelly

900 g | 32 oz ripe green
  gooseberries
petals from 3–4 roses, see note
300 ml | 11 fl oz | 1⅓ cups water
white (granulated) sugar,
  see recipe
few drops rosewater (optional)

1 Put the gooseberries, rose petals and water into a large heavy-based pan.

2 Heat gently to boiling point, then reduce the heat, cover the pan and simmer very gently until the skins are soft, stirring from time to time to prevent the fruit sticking.

3 Ladle the fruit and juices into a scalded jelly bag. Strain the juice through the jelly bag overnight into a bowl. Do not squeeze the bag or the jelly will be cloudy.

4 Measure the juice into a large heavy-based pan and to every 600 ml | 21 fl oz juice allow 450 g | 16 oz sugar.

5 Heat the juice and sugar in the pan and stir over a low heat until the sugar has dissolved completely. Bring to a boil and boil rapidly until setting point is reached. Skim off any scum on the surface and stir in the rosewater if using.

6 Pour into warm sterilised jars. Cover, seal and label.

Grandma's Note
Use heavily scented red or pink petals that are free from chemicals and pesticides – roses bought from a florist aren't suitable. Remove the heel – the white part at the base (this has a bitter flavour) – and wash the flowers gently before use.

Preserves

Preserving was almost a mania with Mrs Bergson ....
When there was nothing to preserve, she began to pickle.

Willa Cather, Death Comes for the Archbishop *(1927)*

Preserved Pears

Prep and cook time: 1 h
Difficulty: easy
Makes: 1–2 kg | 35–71 oz
  preserves

1500 g | 53 oz cooking or
  hard pears, peeled, cored
  and quartered
slightly salted cold water
lemon juice
600 ml | 21 fl oz | 2½ cups
  white distilled vinegar
450 g | 16 oz | 2 cups sugar
½ lemon, finely pared rind
1 tsp ground mixed spice
½ tsp grated nutmeg
4 cinnamon sticks, broken
4 cloves

1 Put the pears into a bowl of slightly salted water with a dash of lemon juice, to prevent them becoming brown.

2 Mix a little of the vinegar with the mixed spice and nutmeg and put the remaining vinegar and the sugar into a pan with the lemon rind.

3 Heat gently until the sugar has dissolved completely, then add the spice mixture and 2 cinnamon sticks and bring to a boil.

4 Rinse the pears and add to the pan.

5 Simmer gently for about 15–20 minutes, until the pears look clear and are tender, but not broken.

6 Remove the pears using a slotted spoon and put into warm sterilised jars with the remaining cinnamon sticks and cloves.

7 Discard the lemon rind and cinnamon sticks from the pan mixture. Boil the liquid in the pan rapidly for about 10–15 minutes until it has thickened to a syrup.

8 Pour over the pears to cover them completely and seal the jars immediately.

Quince Compote with Vanilla

Prep and cook time: 45 min
Difficulty: easy
Makes: 1 kg | 31 oz compote

4 quinces
½ lemon, juice
2 vanilla pods
150 g | 5 oz | ¾ cup brown sugar
1 clove
250 ml | 9 fl oz | 1 cup water
150 ml | 5 fl oz | ⅔ cup dry
  white wine

1 Peel, deseed and cut the
   quinces into wedges.

2 Put the fruit into a bowl
   and drizzle the lemon juice
   over the top.

3 Cut the vanilla pods open
   lengthwise and scrape out
   the seeds.

4 Put the seeds, sugar, clove,
   water and wine into a pan
   and slowly bring to a
   boil, stirring.

5 Add the quince wedges
   and cover. Simmer for
   about 30 minutes until
   tender but not mushy
   (cooking time may vary).

6 Put into hot sterilised jars,
   cover and seal.

Preserved Red Capsicums

Prep and cook time: 25 min
Draining: 12 h
Difficulty: easy
Makes: 1 kg | 31 oz preserves

12 red capsicums (peppers), seeds
  and pith removed, sliced
sea salt
960 ml | 34 fl oz | 4 cups white
  wine vinegar
450 g | 16 oz | 2 cups white
  (granulated) sugar
25 g | 1 oz mustard seeds
1 tsp peppercorns
1 tsp celery seeds

1 Put the capsicums (peppers)
   into a colander over a large
   bowl and sprinkle with a
   generous layer of salt. Cover
   and leave overnight to drain.

2 Rinse the capsicums under
   cold running water, then
   press them to squeeze out
   the excess moisture and dry
   them thoroughly.

3 Put the vinegar, sugar and
   spices into a pan and heat
   slowly, stirring until the sugar
   has dissolved. Bring to a boil
   and simmer for 3 minutes.
   Add the capsicums and
   simmer for a further
   3 minutes.

4 Put into hot sterilised jars,
   making sure the capsicums
   are completely covered with
   the vinegar mixture. Cover,
   seal and label. Store for
   1 month before using.

Green Olives

Prep and cook time: 31–35 days
Difficulty: difficult
Makes: 1 kg | 35 oz olives

First curing:
1000 g | 35 oz green olives
water

Second curing:
3000 ml | 106 fl oz | 13 cups water
80 g | 3 oz sea salt
1 lemon, sliced
2 tbsp dried oregano
500 ml | 18 fl oz | 2 cups white
   wine vinegar
extra virgin olive oil

To serve:
1 red chilli, seeds removed,
   sliced (optional)

1 Crack the olives with a rolling pin or hammer to soften the flesh. Rinse with cold water. Place them in a stoneware, earthenware or glass jar and cover with cold water. Place a large, weighted plate on top to keep the olives submerged and cover. Keep in a cool, dark place for 10–14 days, changing the water each day.

2 Boil the water and dissolve the salt in it. Empty the liquid from the jar in which the olives have been soaking; rinse the olives in cold water and drain well.

3 Put the olives into a container as before and cover the olives with the salt brine. Add the lemon, oregano and vinegar. Pour enough olive oil on top to cover the surface. Cover and store in a cool dark place for 3 weeks.

4 Put the olives and vinegar mixture into cold sterilised jars and seal tightly. Store in the refrigerator and use within 2 months. Garnish with chilli to serve.

Cherry Compote

Prep and cook time: 45 min
Difficulty: easy
Makes: 1 kg | 35 oz compote

1000 g | 35 oz cherries,
  pitted weight
150 ml | 5 fl oz | ⅔ cup water
500 g | 18 oz | 2¼ cups jam
  sugar, see note
½ lemon, juice
4 tsp cherry liqueur or port

1 Put the cherries and water
   into a wide, deep pan and
   bring to a boil. Reduce the
   heat and simmer for about
   15 minutes, stirring
   occasionally, until the fruit
   is starting to soften.

2 Add the sugar, stirring until
   it has dissolved. Add the
   lemon juice and cherry liqueur,
   then bring back to a boil.

3 Boil for about 15 minutes
   until the fruit has collapsed
   a little and the liquid is
   smooth and syrupy.

4 Spoon into hot sterilised
   jars, cover, seal and label.

Grandma's Note
Jam sugar has added pectin.

Fruit Mustard

Prep and cook time: 3 h
Difficulty: medium
Makes: 900 g | 32 oz fruit
mustard

750 g | 26 oz mixed fruit,
e.g. figs, plums, pears,
cherries, quince, apricots, etc.
water
450 g | 16 oz | 2 cups white
(granulated) sugar
½ lemon, juice
120 ml | 4 fl oz | ½ cup dry
white wine
300 ml | 11 fl oz | 1⅓ cups honey
55 g | 2 oz | ½ cup mustard seeds
star anise (optional)

1 Peel the pears if using and slice or chop the other fruits, but leave the cherries whole.

2 Put all the fruit into a large pan and just cover with water. Add the sugar and lemon juice and heat gently until the sugar has dissolved.

3 Bring to a boil, reduce the heat and simmer for 10 minutes.

4 Heat the oven to its lowest setting. Line a large baking tray (sheet) with non-stick baking paper.

5 Remove the fruit from the pan with a slotted spoon (reserve the syrup) and place on the baking tray. Dry the fruit in the oven until dry to the touch.

6 Add the wine and honey to the syrup in the pan and bring to a boil over a low heat. Boil for 5 minutes.

7 Warm the mustard seeds gently in another pan until they begin to pop. Stir the mustard seeds into the honey mixture, mixing well and remove from the heat.

8 Put the fruit into hot sterilised jars and pour over the syrup. Add a star anise. Cover and seal tightly and leave to cool. Store in the refrigerator for up to 2 weeks.

Oranges and Peaches with Vanilla

Prep and cook time: 35 min
Difficulty: medium
Makes: 700 g | 25 oz preserves

350 g | 12 oz oranges, peeled and
   cut into segments
300 ml | 11 fl oz | 1⅓ cups water
225 ml | 8 fl oz | 1 cup white
   wine vinegar
225 g | 8 oz | 1 cup brown sugar
2 cloves
1 vanilla pod
350 g | 12 oz peaches, skinned
   and quartered

1 Put the orange segments in a pan with the water and bring
   to a simmer. Simmer very gently until tender. Drain well and
   reserve the cooking liquid.

2 Heat the cooking liquid, vinegar, sugar, cloves and vanilla pod
   until the sugar has dissolved. Bring to a boil and boil rapidly
   for 5 minutes.

3 Add the oranges and peaches and simmer very gently until the
   fruit is tender but still whole.

4 Spoon the fruit into warm sterilised jars.

5 Boil the syrup until thickened and syrupy, and pour over the
   fruit with the vanilla pod and cloves. Cover, seal and label.
   Eat within 3 months.

Plums in Red Wine

Prep and cook time: 45 min
Difficulty: easy
Makes: 450 g | 16 oz preserves

450 g | 16 oz small plums
300 ml | 11 fl oz | 1⅓ cups red
  wine vinegar
225 g | 8 oz | 1 cup white
  (granulated) sugar
½ lemon, finely pared rind
small piece root ginger
  (gingerroot), bruised
4 cloves
1 cinnamon stick, broken

1 Prick the plums all over
   with a darning needle and
   place in a heavy-based pan.

2 Cover with vinegar and add
   the sugar.

3 Add the lemon rind and
   spices to the pan. Heat
   gently, stirring, until the
   sugar has dissolved
   completely, then bring
   to a boil.

4 Reduce the heat and
   simmer very gently until the
   fruit is tender – but don't
   let the skins break.

5 Remove the fruit, lemon
   rind, cloves and cinnamon
   with a slotted spoon and
   pack into warm sterilised
   jars. Discard the ginger.

6 Boil the liquid rapidly for
   5 minutes, then pour
   immediately over the plums
   to cover completely. Cover
   and seal tightly.

Preserved Kumquats

Prep and cook time: 1 h 30 min
Difficulty: easy
Makes: 25–30 kumquats

25–30 kumquats
500 ml | 18 fl oz | 2 cups water,
  plus more to cover
450 g | 16 oz | 2 cups white
  (granulated) sugar
1 vanilla pod, split

1 Put the kumquats into a large
   pan and add just enough
   water to cover the fruit.

2 Bring to a boil and when foam
   forms on the surface reduce
   the heat and boil gently for
   a further 10 minutes. Drain
   and set aside.

3 Pour the 500 ml | 18 fl oz |
   2 cups water into a large pan
   and add the sugar. Heat
   gently, stirring, until the
   sugar has dissolved.

4 Add the kumquats and
   vanilla pod and bring to a
   boil. Reduce the heat and
   simmer, stirring occasionally
   until the kumquats are
   transparent and soft.
   Discard the vanilla pod.

5 Spoon the kumquats and
   syrup into hot sterilised jars,
   cover and seal tightly. Leave
   to cool, then store in the
   refrigerator for up to 2 weeks.

Vanilla Chestnuts

Prep and cook time: 3 h
First standing: 8 h
Second standing: 12 h
Difficulty: difficult
Makes: 900 g | 32 oz preserves

700 g | 25 oz chestnuts
boiling water, see recipe
water
2 tsp lemon juice
white (granulated) sugar,
   see recipe
2 vanilla pods

1 Slit each chestnut shell across 1 side with a sharp knife. Put into a pan and add boiling water to cover. Boil for 1 minute. Drain well and remove the shells and furry lining while the nuts are hot.

2 Place the shelled chestnuts in a bowl and cover with cold water. Stir in the lemon juice and leave to stand for 8 hours.

3 Drain the chestnuts and cover with plenty of boiling water. Bring to a boil, then reduce the heat and simmer very gently for 1–2 hours until the chestnuts are tender.

4 Drain the chestnuts and weigh them, then set aside.

5 Add the same weight of sugar and the same volume of water and the vanilla pods to the pan. Stir over a low heat until the sugar has dissolved. Increase the heat and bring to a boil. Add the chestnuts and bring to a boil again, then remove from the heat and allow to cool. Cover and stand overnight.

6 Bring the chestnuts and syrup to a boil again. Remove the chestnuts with a slotted spoon and place in hot sterilised jars with the vanilla pods. If the syrup is not thick enough, continue to boil until thickened.

7 Pour over the chestnuts, cover and seal tightly.

Eggplant with Thyme

Prep and cook time: 20 min
Standing: 30 min
Difficulty: easy
Makes: 2 kg | 71 oz preserves

2000 g | 71 oz eggplants
    (aubergines), sliced
4 tbsp salt
1200 ml | 41 fl oz | 5 cups white
    wine vinegar
2 tbsp white (granulated) sugar
125 ml | 4½ fl oz | ½ cup olive oil
2 tbsp thyme
thyme sprigs

1 Put the eggplants
   (aubergines) in a colander
   and sprinkle with the salt.
   Place over a bowl or in the
   sink, to drain for 30 minutes.

2 Heat the vinegar and sugar
   in a pan over a low heat
   until the sugar has dissolved.

3 Bring to a boil and add
   the eggplants and boil
   for 5 minutes. Do not
   overcook. Drain well,
   reserving the cooking liquid.

4 Add the oil and thyme to
   the eggplants and toss well.
   Pack into warm sterilised
   jars, pressing the eggplants
   mixture to the bottom of
   the jars to release their juice.
   Pour over the reserved
   cooking liquid.

5 Add the thyme sprigs and
   seal tightly. Store in a cool,
   dark place for 4 weeks
   before use.

Sweet and Sour Pickled Onions

Prep and cook time: 25 min
Difficulty: easy
Makes: 1 × 1000 ml | 35 fl oz |
* 4 cup jar*

500 g | 18 oz pearl onions or
  small pickling onions
400 ml | 14 fl oz | 1⅔ cups white
  wine vinegar
20 g | ¾ oz sea salt
100 g | 3½ oz | ½ cup
  brown sugar
2 tsp black peppercorns
1 tsp cloves
2 dried chillies

1 Cover the onions with
   boiling water, remove their
   skins and blanch in boiling
   water for 2 minutes.
   Remove and leave to drain.

2 Put the vinegar, salt, sugar,
   peppercorns, cloves and
   chillies into a pan and bring
   to a boil.

3 Pack the onions into hot
   sterilised jars and pour over
   the hot vinegar mixture,
   so that all the onions are
   covered. Cover and seal,
   and leave to stand for
   2 weeks before eating.

Fig Preserve

Prep and cook time: 45 min
Difficulty: easy
Makes: 750 g | 26 oz preserves

450 g | 16 oz figs, chopped
2 tbsp water
450 g | 16 oz | 2 cups white
   (granulated) sugar
2 tbsp lemon juice

1 Put the figs and water into
   a large pan. bring to a
   boil, then reduce the heat
   and simmer until the figs
   are soft.

2 Add the sugar and lemon
   juice and stir over a low
   heat until the sugar has
   dissolved. Bring to a boil
   and boil rapidly until
   setting point is reached.

3 Remove from the heat and
   allow to cool slightly. Stir
   once and spoon into hot
   sterilised jars. Cover, seal
   and label.

Pickled Garlic

Prep and cook time: 20 min
Difficulty: easy
Makes: 1 kg | 35 oz pickled
garlic

12 heads garlic, separated
   into cloves
boiling water
625 ml | 22 fl oz | 2½ cups white
   wine vinegar
250 ml | 9 fl oz | 1 cup dry
   white wine
1 tbsp sea salt
1 tbsp white (granulated) sugar

1 Put the garlic cloves into a
   pan of rapidly boiling water
   for 30 seconds. Immediately
   immerse in cold water,
   drain and peel the cloves.
   Set aside.

2 Put the vinegar, wine, salt
   and sugar in a large pan.
   Heat gently, stirring, until
   the sugar has dissolved.
   Bring to a boil and boil
   gently for 1 minute. Remove
   from the heat, add the garlic
   cloves and stir well.

3 Remove the garlic with a
   slotted spoon and pack into
   hot sterilised jars. Pour in
   the hot vinegar, making
   sure the garlic is completely
   covered. Seal tightly. Store
   in the refrigerator for
   2–3 weeks before using.

Grandma's Note
You can leave the garlic unpeeled.

Chutneys
& Relishes

Chutney is marvellous. I'm mad about it. To me, it's very imperial.

Diana Vreeland (1903–1989)

Pineapple Chutney with Chilli

Prep and cook time: 1 h 15 min
Difficulty: easy
Makes: 1 kg | 35 oz chutney

3 tbsp olive oil
2 onions, finely chopped
1 tsp mustard seeds, toasted
½ tsp ground turmeric
½ tsp ground ginger
1 clove garlic, finely chopped
1 red chilli, seeds removed,
    chopped
1 pineapple, peeled, cored and
    cut into chunks
1 sprig rosemary
1 tbsp honey
100 ml | 3½ fl oz | 7 tbsp
    cider vinegar
120 g | 4 oz | ½ cup brown sugar
salt and pepper

1 Heat the oil in a frying pan and cook the onions over a low heat until softened.

2 Add the mustard seeds, spices, garlic and chilli and cook for 2 minutes.

3 Put into a large heavy-based pan and add the remaining ingredients. Stir over a low heat until the sugar has dissolved, then reduce the heat and simmer for 40–60 minutes until thick. Remove the rosemary. Season to taste with salt and pepper.

4 Spoon into hot sterilised jars. Cover, seal and label.

Plum Chutney

Prep and cook time: 1 h 25 min
Difficulty: medium
Makes: 2–3 kg | 71–106 oz
  chutney

1000 g | 35 oz ripe plums,
  pitted weight
225 g | 8 oz apples, roughly
  chopped
1 onion, finely chopped
225 g | 8 oz | 1½ cups sultanas
  (golden raisins)
225 g | 8 oz | 1 cup brown sugar
1 tbsp salt
1 tsp ground ginger
½ tsp ground cloves
1 tsp ground allspice
600 ml | 21 fl oz | 2½ cups red
  wine vinegar

1 Mix together the plums, apples, onion, sultanas (golden raisins) and sugar in a bowl.

2 Put the salt and spices in a pan with the vinegar and bring slowly to a boil over a low heat. Add the fruit and sugar mixture, stir well and bring to a boil again. Reduce the heat and simmer steadily until thick. To test when the chutney is cooked make a channel across the surface with a wooden spoon: if the impression lasts for a few seconds and does not fill up with vinegar it is ready.

3 Remove the pan from the heat. Spoon the chutney into warm sterilised jars, seal and label.

Spicy Berry and Kiwifruit Relish with Chillies

Prep and cook time: 1 h 10 min
Difficulty: easy
Makes: 900 g | 32 oz relish

100 g | 3½ oz gooseberries
450 g | 16 oz kiwifruit, peeled
  and chopped
1 onion, chopped
3 chillies, seeds removed, sliced
1 tbsp grated root ginger (gingerroot)
225 g | 8 oz | 1 cup brown sugar
250 ml | 9 fl oz | 1 cup
  cider vinegar

1 Put all the ingredients into a large heavy-based pan. Heat gently, stirring, until the sugar has dissolved.

2 Increase the heat and bring to a boil. Reduce the heat and simmer until the mixture is thick and pulpy.

3 Spoon into hot sterilised jars, cover, seal and label.

Tomato Chutney

Prep and cook time: 1 h
Difficulty: easy
Makes: 2 kg | 71 oz chutney

1000 g | 35 oz firm ripe tomatoes,
    skinned and chopped
450 g | 16 oz onions,
    finely chopped
450 g | 16 oz cooking apples,
    peeled and cored weight, finely
    chopped
450 ml | 16 fl oz | 2 cups vinegar
1 tsp ground ginger
1 tsp ground mixed spice
350 g | 12 oz | 1¾ cups white
    (granulated) sugar
300 g | 11 oz | 2 cups sultanas
    (golden raisins)
salt and pepper

1 Put all the ingredients except
   the sugar, sultanas (golden
   raisins), salt and pepper into
   a large heavy-based pan.

2 Bring to a boil, then reduce
   the heat and simmer steadily
   for about 20 minutes, stirring
   occasionally until thick.

3 Remove from the heat and
   stir in the sugar until
   dissolved completely. Add
   the sultanas and season to
   taste. Stir well, over a low
   heat, then increase the heat
   and simmer steadily, for
   about 20 minutes, stirring
   occasionally until the
   mixture is very thick.

4 Remove the pan from the
   heat. Spoon the chutney
   into warm sterilised jars,
   seal and label.

Rose Hip Chutney

Prep and cook time: 50 min
Standing: 12 h
Difficulty: medium
Makes: 1 kg | 35 oz chutney

300 ml | 11 fl oz | 1⅓ cups chopped
   rose hips, seeds removed
600 ml | 21 fl oz | 2½ cups
   cider vinegar
225 g | 8 oz | 1⅓ cups sultanas
   (golden raisins)
675 g | 24 oz apples, peeled
   and chopped
2 tsp ground ginger
½ tsp cayenne pepper
½ tsp ground cloves
1 clove garlic, finely chopped
225 g | 8 oz | 1 cup white
   (granulated) sugar
2 tbsp lemon juice
2 tbsp orange juice
2 tsp grated orange zest

1 Put the rose hips and
   vinegar into a bowl. Mix
   well, cover and leave to
   stand overnight.

2 Put the mixture into a large
   pan with the remaining
   ingredients and heat
   slowly until the sugar
   has dissolved.

3 Bring to a boil and cook
   until the mixture is thick
   and pulpy.

4 Spoon into hot sterilised
   jars, cover, seal and label.

Lime Chutney

Prep and cook time: 2 h
Standing: 48 h
Difficulty: easy
Makes: 600 g | 21 oz chutney

10 limes
2 tbsp salt
150 g | 5 oz | 1 cup sultanas
  (golden raisins)
3 tbsp oil
2 tsp ground cumin
1 tsp ground coriander
1 tsp chilli flakes
½ tsp ground black pepper
3 cloves garlic, finely chopped
5 cm | 2" piece ginger (gingerroot),
  finely chopped
310 ml | 11 fl oz | 1¼ cups malt
  vinegar
1000 g | 35 oz | 4 cups brown sugar
2 cinnamon sticks
2 vanilla pods
4 star anise

1 Cut each lime into 8 wedges. Place in large bowl, sprinkle with the salt and stir well. Cover and leave to stand for 48 hours in a cool dark place, stirring occasionally.

2 Drain, rinse well and mix with the sultanas.

3 Heat the oil in a frying pan and add the cumin, coriander, chilli flakes, black pepper, garlic and ginger (gingerroot). Cook for 2–3 minutes until aromatic.

4 Put the spices into a large pan with the lime and sultanas (golden raisins), vinegar and sugar. Bring to a boil, stirring until the sugar dissolves.

5 Reduce the heat and simmer for about 1½ hours, stirring occasionally, until thickened. Spoon into warm, sterilised jars. Add the whole spices to the jars, seal and label.

Mixed Fruit Chutney

Prep and cook time: 1 h 30 min
Difficulty: easy
Makes: 2 kg | 71 oz chutney

450 g | 16 oz onions, finely
  chopped
300 ml | 11 fl oz | 1⅓ cups white
  malt vinegar
450 g | 16 oz cooking apples,
  peeled and cored weight, diced
400 g | 14 oz pears, peeled and
  cored weight, diced
50 g | 1¾ oz | ⅓ cup sultanas
  (golden raisins)
110 g | 4 oz | ¾ cup chopped
  dried apricots
350 g | 12 oz | 2½ cups
  brown sugar
salt and pepper
1–2 tbsp coriander seeds, bruised

1 Put the onions and half the vinegar into a large heavy-based pan and bring to a boil.

2 Reduce the heat and simmer gently for 10 minutes.

3 Add the apples, pears and sultanas (golden raisins) to the pan with the remaining vinegar, apricots, sugar and a sprinkling of salt and pepper.

4 Stir over a low heat until the sugar has dissolved completely, then increase the heat and simmer steadily, for about 40–60 minutes, stirring occasionally until the mixture is very thick. Stir in the coriander seeds.

5 Spoon into hot sterilised jars, seal and label. Leave to mature for at least 3 months in a cool, dry, dark place.

Sweetcorn Relish

Prep and cook time: 35 min
Difficulty: easy
Makes: 1 kg | 35 oz relish

4 sweetcorn cobs
1 red capsicums (pepper), seeds
  removed and diced
1 green capsicums (pepper), seeds
  removed and diced
1 stick celery, thinly sliced
1 red chilli, seeds removed and
  chopped (optional)
1 onion, chopped peeled and sliced
450 ml | 16 fl oz | 2 cups white
  wine vinegar
225 g | 8 oz | 1 cup white
  (granulated) sugar
2 tsp salt
2 tsp mustard powder
½ tsp ground turmeric

1 Strip the kernels from the
   cobs with a sharp knife. Put
   into a pan of boiling water
   and cook for 2 minutes,
   then drain well.

2 Put the sweetcorn kernels
   and the remaining
   ingredients into a large pan.
   Heat gently, stirring until
   the sugar has dissolved,
   then bring to a boil, stirring
   frequently and cook for
   15–20 minutes until thick
   but moist. It should be a
   spoonable consistency, but
   not as thick as chutney.

3 Spoon into warm sterilised
   jars, cover, seal and label.

Green Apple Chutney with Ginger

Prep and cook time: 1 h
Difficulty: easy
Makes: 1–2 kg | 35–71 oz
   chutney

450 g | 16 oz onions,
   finely chopped
300 ml | 11 fl oz | 1⅓ cups
   cider vinegar
900 g | 32 oz cooking apples,
   peeled and cored weight, diced
350 g | 12 oz | 1½ cups white
   (granulated) sugar
1 tbsp grated root ginger
   (gingerroot)
110 g | 4 oz stem ginger
   (gingerroot), thinly sliced
salt and pepper

1 Put the onions and half the
   vinegar into a large pan and
   bring to a boil. Reduce the
   heat and simmer gently for
   10 minutes.

2 Add the apples, remaining
   vinegar, sugar and ginger
   (gingerroot). Stir over a low
   heat until the sugar has
   dissolved, then cook gently,
   stirring occasionly until
   thick and pulpy. Season to
   taste with salt and pepper.

3 Spoon into hot sterilised
   jars, cover, seal and label.

Onion Chutney with Thyme

Prep and cook time: 1 h 40 min
Difficulty: easy
Makes: 1 kg | 35 oz chutney

140 g | 5 oz | ⅔ cup butter
4 tbsp olive oil
2000 g | 71 oz red onions,
  thinly sliced
4 garlic cloves, finely chopped
140 g | 5 oz | ⅔ cup white
  (granulated) sugar
1 tbsp thyme leaves
salt and pepper
750 ml | 25 fl oz | 3 cups red wine
350 ml | 12 fl oz | 1½ cups red
  wine vinegar
200 ml | 7 fl oz | ⅞ cup port

To garnish:
thyme sprigs

1 Heat the butter and oil in a
   large heavy-based pan. Add
   the onion and garlic, then
   sprinkle over the sugar,
   thyme and a sprinkling of
   salt and pepper. Stir well
   and reduce the heat.

2 Cook uncovered for
   40–50 minutes, stirring
   occasionally until the onions
   are very soft and sticky.

3 Pour in the wine, vinegar and
   port and simmer uncovered
   for 25–30 minutes, stirring
   occasionally, until most of
   the liquid has evaporated.
   Set aside to cool until warm.

4 Spoon into warm sterilised
   jars, cover, seal and label.
   Serve garnished with thyme
   sprigs.

Red Chutney

Prep and cook time: 45 min
Difficulty: easy
Makes: 1 kg | 35 oz chutney

900 g | 32 oz red capsicums
   (peppers), seeds removed,
   chopped
450 g | 16 oz red onions, chopped
450 ml | 16 fl oz | 2 cups red
   wine vinegar
2 tsp salt
1 tsp white peppercorns
1 tsp celery seeds
225 g | 8 oz | 1 cup brown sugar

1 Put the capsicums
   (peppers), onions, vinegar,
   salt, peppercorns and celery
   seeds into a large heavy-
   based pan. Bring to a boil,
   then reduce the heat and
   simmer gently, stirring
   ocassionally until the
   vegetables are tender.

2 Add the sugar and stir over
   a low heat until the sugar
   has dissolved. Increase the
   heat and cook the mixture
   steadily until thick.

3 Spoon into hot sterilised
   jars. Cover, seal and label.

Apricot and Plum Purée

Prep and cook time: 45 min
Soaking: 2 h
Difficulty: easy
Makes: 750 g | 26 oz purée

225 g | 8 oz ready-to-eat
  dried apricots
225 g | 8 oz ready-to-eat prunes
600 ml | 21 fl oz | 2½ cups water
1 vanilla pod
1 cinnamon stick, broken
4 tbsp lemon juice
450 g | 16 oz | 2 cups white
  (granulated) sugar

1 Put the apricots, prunes,
   water, vanilla pod and
   cinnamon stick into a
   bowl. Cover and leave to
   soak for 2 hours.

2 Strain the liquid into a large
   pan. Chop the apricots and
   prunes and add to the pan
   with the vanilla pod,
   cinnamon stick, lemon
   juice and sugar.

3 Heat gently until the sugar
   has dissolved. Bring to a
   boil, then reduce the heat
   and simmer gently until
   the fruit is just tender.
   Remove the vanilla pod
   and cinnamon.

4 Spoon into hot sterilised
   jars. Cover, seal and label.

Mango and Ginger Chutney

Prep and cook time: 1 h 15 min
Difficulty: easy
Makes: 1 kg | 35 oz chutney

1000 g | 35 oz mangoes, peeled
  and chopped
1 onion, finely chopped
½ tsp salt
350 ml | 12 fl oz | 1½ cups white
  wine vinegar
225 g | 8 oz | 1 cup brown sugar
5 cm | 2" piece root ginger
  (gingerroot), grated
50 g | 1¾ oz | ⅓ cup sultanas
  (golden raisins)
110 g | 4 oz stem ginger
  (gingerroot), finely chopped
1 cinnamon stick
¼ tsp cayenne pepper
½ tsp grated nutmeg

1 Put the mangoes, onions,
   salt and vinegar into a large
   pan and cook gently until
   beginning to soften.

2 Add the sugar and heat
   gently until the sugar has
   dissolved. Bring to a boil.
   Add the remaining
   ingredients and bring to
   a boil, stirring.

3 Cook gently for 40–60
   minutes until thick and the
   vinegar has been absorbed.
   Discard the cinnamon stick.

4 Spoon into hot sterilised
   jars, cover, seal and label.

Cranberry Chutney

Prep and cook time: 50 min
Difficulty: easy
Makes: 1 kg | 35 oz chutney

450 g | 16 oz cooking apples,
  peeled and cored weight,
  roughly chopped
450 g | 16 oz | 4 cups cranberries
1 onion, finely chopped
1 tsp allspice berries
1 tsp cardamom seeds
1 tsp ground mixed spice
300 ml | 11 fl oz | 1⅓ cups
  cider vinegar
350 g | 12 oz | 1½ cups white
  (granulated) sugar
salt and pepper

1 Put the apples, cranberries
   and onions into a large
   heavy-based pan.

2 Tie the whole spices in
   muslin and put into the pan
   with the mixed spice and
   vinegar. Cover the pan
   tightly and and cook gently
   for 15 minutes.

3 Stir well and simmer
   uncovered until the fruit is
   soft. Add the sugar and stir
   until dissolved.

4 Cook steadily until the
   chutney is thick. Season to
   taste with salt and pepper.
   Remove the muslin bag.

5 Spoon into hot sterilised
   jars, cover, seal and label.

Apple Chutney with Raisins

Prep and cook time: 1 h 30 min
Difficulty: easy
Makes: 1–2 kg | 35–71 oz chutney

450 g | 16 oz onions,
  finely chopped
300 ml | 11 fl oz | 1⅓ cups white
  malt vinegar
1000 g | 35 oz cooking apples,
  peeled and cored weight, chopped
2 tsp cardamom seeds, crushed
350 g | 12 oz | 1½ cups
  brown sugar
110 g | 4 oz | ¾ cup raisins
  or sultanas (golden raisins)
salt and pepper

1 Put the onions and half the
   vinegar into a large heavy-
   based pan and bring to a boil.

2 Reduce the heat and simmer
   gently for 10 minutes.

3 Add the apples to the pan
   with the remaining vinegar,
   cardamom seeds, sugar,
   raisins or sultanas (golden
   raisins) and a sprinkling of
   salt and pepper.

4 Stir over a low heat until
   the sugar has dissolved
   completely, then increase the
   heat and simmer steadily, for
   about 40–60 minutes,
   stirring occasionally until the
   mixture is very thick.

5 Spoon into hot sterilised
   jars, seal and label.

6 Leave to mature for up to
   3 months in a cool, dry,
   dark place.

Apple and Celery Relish with Capers

Prep and cook time: 1 h
Difficulty: easy
Makes: 1 kg | 35 oz relish

375 ml | 13 fl oz | 1½ cups
    cider vinegar
1 tsp salt
225 g | 8 oz | 1 cup white
    (granulated) sugar
½ tsp ground ginger
400 g | 14 oz celery, chopped
400 g | 14 oz cooking apples,
    peeled, cored and diced
2 tbsp capers, rinsed

1 Put all the ingredients
   except the capers into a
   large heavy-based pan.
   Heat gently, stirring, until
   the sugar has dissolved.

2 Increase the heat and bring
   to a boil. Reduce the heat
   and simmer until the apples
   and celery are tender and
   the mixture is thick. Stir in
   the capers.

3 Spoon into hot sterilised
   jars, cover, seal and label.

Green Tomato Chutney

Prep and cook time: 2 h
Difficulty: medium
Makes: 2 kg | 71 oz chutney

1500 g | 53 oz green tomatoes,
   roughly chopped
450 g | 16 oz cooking apples,
   peeled, cored and chopped
675 g | 24 oz shallots or onions,
   finely chopped
2 cloves garlic (optional)
225 g | 8 oz | 1½ cups sultanas
   (golden raisins)
1 tsp salt
½ tsp cayenne pepper
15 g | ½ oz root ginger
   (gingerroot), bruised
600 ml | 21 fl oz | 2½ cups vinegar
450 g | 16 oz | 2 cups brown sugar

To garnish:
1 red chilli, finely chopped
thinly sliced onion

1 Put the tomatoes, apples, shallots or onions, garlic and sultanas (golden raisins) in a large heavy-based pan with the salt and cayenne pepper.

2 Tie the ginger (gingerroot) loosely in a piece of muslin and add to the pan.

3 Stir in a little of the vinegar and cook gently over a low heat for about 1 hour until the vegetables and fruit are soft, stirring from time to time. Remove from the heat and stir in the sugar and remaining vinegar.

4 When the sugar has dissolved completely, return to the heat and bring to a boil. Reduce the heat and simmer gently for 1–1½ hours until thick.

5 Spoon into hot sterilised jars, seal and label. Serve garnished with chilli and thinly sliced onion.

Tapenades, Pesto, Oils & Vinegars

Vinegar, the son of wine.

Proverb

Caper Tapenade

Prep and cook time: 15 min
Difficulty: easy
Makes: 300 g | 11 oz tapenade

250 g | 9 oz green olives, pitted
  and chopped
1 lemon, juice
3 tbsp capers, drained
1 clove garlic
3 tbsp chopped flat leaf parsley
120 ml | 4 fl oz | ½ cup extra
  virgin olive oil
sea salt
freshly ground black pepper

1 Put the olives in a food
   processor with the lemon
   juice, capers, garlic and
   parsley. Blend until
   just combined.

2 Pour in sufficient olive oil
   to make a purée. Season to
   taste with salt and pepper.

3 Spoon into cold sterilised
   jars and store in the
   refrigerator for up to
   1 week.

Olive Oil with Herbs and Lemon

Prep and cook time: 15 min
Difficulty: easy
Makes: 650 ml | 23 fl oz |
    2⅔ cups oil

2 lemons, pared zest only
15–20 sprigs thyme
650 ml | 23 fl oz | 2⅔ cups extra
    virgin olive oil

1 Put the lemon zest into
   cold sterilised glass bottles
   or jars.

2 Bruise the thyme a little, to
   release the flavour and put
   into the bottles.

3 Pour in the oil to
   completely cover the lemon
   and herbs. Seal tightly and
   leave to infuse for a few
   days before using.

4 Store in a cool, dry place
   and use within 1 month.

Parsley and Walnut Pesto

Prep and cook time: 15 min
Difficulty: easy
Makes: 250 g | 9 oz pesto

40 g | 1½ oz | 1½ cups chopped
   flat leaf parsley leaves
55 g | 2 oz | ½ cup
   chopped walnuts
2 cloves garlic, chopped
35 g | 1¼ oz | ⅓ cup grated
   Parmesan cheese
sea salt
freshly ground pepper
125 ml | 4½ fl oz | ½ cup extra
   virgin olive oil

1 Put the parsley, walnuts,
   garlic, Parmesan and a little
   salt and pepper in a food
   processor. Blend until
   smooth, scraping down the
   side occasionally.

2 With the motor running
   gradually pour in most
   of the olive oil until
   well blended.

3 Spoon into cold sterilised
   jars. Pour a little of the
   remaining oil over the top
   and seal tightly. Store in
   the refrigerator for up to
   1 month.

Pickled Garlic with Rosemary

Prep and cook time: 20 min
Standing: 24 h
Difficulty: easy
Makes: 250 g | 9 oz pickled garlic

125 ml | 4½ fl oz | ½ cup white
  wine vinegar
125 ml | 4½ fl oz | ½ cup dry
  white wine
2 sprigs rosemary
10 black peppercorns
1 bay leaf
2 tsp white (granulated) sugar
½ tsp sea salt
2 heads garlic, separated into
  cloves and peeled

1 Put all the ingredients
   except the garlic into a
   large pan. Heat gently,
   stirring, until the sugar
   has dissolved.

2 Increase the heat and bring
   to a boil. Cook steadily for
   5 minutes, then add the
   garlic. Bring to a boil, then
   cover and remove from the
   heat. Leave to stand at
   room temperature for
   24 hours. Remove the
   peppercorns and bay leaf.

3 Bring to a boil again, then
   spoon into hot sterilised
   jars. Seal tightly and leave
   to cool. Store in the
   refrigerator for 1 week
   before using.

Strawberry Vinegar

Prep and cook time: 20 min
Standing: 72 h
Straining: 12 h
Difficulty: medium
Makes: 600 ml | 21 fl oz |
  2½ cups vinegar

450 g | 16 oz strawberries, plus
  extra to finish
600 ml | 21 fl oz | 2½ cups white
  wine vinegar
white (granulated) sugar,
  see recipe

1 Crush the fruit in a large bowl and stir in the vinegar. Cover and leave to stand for 3 days in the refrigerator, stirring frequently.

2 Ladle the fruit and juices into a scalded jelly bag. Strain the juice through the jelly bag overnight into a bowl. Do not squeeze the bag or the vinegar will be cloudy.

3 Measure the juice into a large heavy-based pan and to every 600 ml | 21 fl oz juice allow 225 g | 8 oz sugar.

4 Heat the juice and sugar in a pan and stir over a low heat until the sugar has dissolved completely. Bring to a boil and boil rapidly for 5 minutes, skimming off any scum. Add the extra strawberries and simmer for 5 minutes.

5 Spoon the strawberries into hot sterilised jars and pour in the hot vinegar. Cover, seal and label.

Thyme and Garlic Infused Oil

Prep and cook time: 20 min
Standing: 24 h
Difficulty: easy
Makes: 250 ml | 9 fl oz | 1 cup oil

125 ml | 4½ fl oz | ½ cup white
wine vinegar
125 ml | 4½ fl oz | ½ cup dry
white wine
4 sprigs thyme
2 cloves
2 tsp sugar
½ tsp sea salt
2 heads garlic, separated into
cloves and peeled

1 Put all the ingredients
except the garlic into a large
pan. Heat gently, stirring,
until the sugar has dissolved.

2 Increase the heat and bring
to a boil. Cook steadily for
5 minutes, then add the
garlic. Bring to a boil, then
cover and remove from the
heat. Leave to stand at
room temperature for
24 hours. Remove 1 clove.

3 Bring to a boil again, then
spoon into hot sterilised
jars. Seal tightly and leave
to cool. Store in the
refrigerator for 1 week
before using.

Tarragon Oil

Prep and cook time: 10 min
Difficulty: easy
Makes: 600 ml | 21 fl oz |
2½ cups oil

12–15 sprigs tarragon
600 ml | 21 fl oz | 2½ cups extra
virgin olive oil

1 Bruise the tarragon a little
   to release the flavour and
   put into cold sterilised glass
   bottles or jars.

2 Pour in the oil to
   completely cover the
   tarragon. Seal tightly and
   leave to infuse for a few
   days before using.

3 Store in a cool, dry place
   and use within 1 month.

Rose Vinegar

Prep and cook time: 15 min
Difficulty: easy
Makes: 600 ml | 21 fl oz |
  2½ cups vinegar

600 ml | 21 fl oz | 2½ cups white
  wine vinegar
55 g | 2 oz | ¼ cup white
  (granulated) sugar
2½ cups scented rose petals

1 Put the vinegar and sugar
   into a pan and heat slowly,
   stirring, until the sugar has
   dissolved. Cover and leave
   to become cold.

2 Put the petals into cold
   sterilised bottles or jars and
   pour over the cold vinegar,
   making sure the rose petals
   are completely covered.

3 Seal tightly and leave for
   3–4 weeks before using.

Grandma's Note
*Use heavily scented red or pink petals that
are free from chemicals and pesticides –
roses bought from a florist aren't suitable.
Remove the heel – the white part at the
base (this has a bitter flavour) – and wash
the flowers gently before use.*

Apple Vinegar

Prep and cook time: 25 min
Standing: 12 h
Difficulty: easy
Makes: 500 ml | 18 fl oz |
  2 cups vinegar

500 ml | 18 fl oz | 2 cups
  cider vinegar
30 g | 1 oz dried apples, chopped
2 bay leaves
1 cinnamon stick, broken
175 g | 6 oz | ¾ cup white
  (granulated) sugar

1 Mix together the vinegar,
  apples, bay leaves and
  cinnamon. Stir well,
  cover and leave to stand
  for 12 hours.

2 Put the vinegar mixture
  into a pan and add the
  sugar. Heat slowly,
  stirring until the sugar has
  dissolved. Bring to a boil
  and cook steadily for
  10 minutes.

3 Strain into hot sterilised
  bottles or jars and seal tightly.

Traditional Pesto

Prep and cook time: 20 min
Difficulty: easy
Makes: 300 g | 11 oz pesto

2 cloves garlic, chopped
1 pinch salt
110 g | 4 oz basil leaves
50 g | 1¾ oz | ½ cup toasted
    pine nuts
50 g | 1¾ oz | ¼ cup
    parmesan cheese
175–220 ml | 6–8 fl oz | ¾–⅞ cup
    extra virgin olive oil

1 Pound the garlic with the salt and basil leaves in a pestle and mortar.

2 Add the pine nuts and pound again. Put into a bowl and add half the cheese.

3 Stir gently and add the olive oil, a tablespoon at a time, and pound until fully incorporated and the mixture is a smooth paste. Add the remaining cheese.

4 Spoon into cold sterilised jars and leave to settle. The oil may rise to the top, but if not, add a thin film of oil on top to preserve the pesto. Store in the refrigerator and use withing 2 weeks.

Wild Garlic Pesto

Prep and cook time: 20 min
Difficulty: easy
Makes: 300 g | 11 oz pesto

55 g | 2 oz | ½ cup
   chopped walnuts
100 g | 3½ oz wild garlic leaves
1 shallot, chopped
150 ml | 5 fl oz | ⅔ cup extra
   virgin olive oil, plus extra
   to cover
35 g | 1¼ oz | ⅓ cup grated
   Parmesan cheese
½ tsp sea salt
¼ tsp freshly ground pepper
½ tsp white (granulated) sugar

1 Heat the oven to 180°C
   (160°C fan | 350°F | gas 4).
   Place the walnuts on a
   baking tray and put in the
   oven for 5–6 minutes until
   lightly toasted and golden.
   Set aside to cool.

2 Put all the ingredients
   except the olive oil in a food
   processor. Blend until
   smooth, scraping down the
   sides occasionally.

3 With the motor running,
   gradually pour in the olive
   oil until well blended.

4 Spoon into cold sterilised
   jars. Pour a little more oil
   over the top and seal tightly.
   Store in the refrigerator for
   up to 2 weeks.

Aioli, Black and Green Tapenades

Prep and cook time: 35 min
Difficulty: easy
Makes: 900 g | 32 oz total

For the aioli:
3 cloves garlic, crushed
½ tsp salt
2 egg yolks
½ tsp Dijon mustard
2 tbsp lemon juice
300 ml | 11 fl oz | 1⅓ cups extra
   virgin olive oil
sea salt
freshly ground black pepper

For the black olive tapenade:
250 g | 9 oz black olives, pitted
2 tbsp capers, drained and rinsed
2 cloves garlic, crushed
3 tbsp extra virgin olive oil, plus
   extra to cover

For the green olive tapenade:
6 small anchovy fillets
175 g | 6 oz green olives, pitted
2 cloves garlic, crushed
1 lemon, juice
2 tbsp chopped flat leaf parsley
85–100 ml | 3–3½ fl oz | 6–7 tbsp
   extra virgin olive oil, plus extra
   to cover

For the aioli:

1 Put the garlic, salt, egg yolks, mustard and lemon juice in a food processor.

2 With the motor running, add the oil in a thin steady stream and blend until the aioli thickens. Season to taste with salt and pepper.

3 Spoon into cold sterilised jars. Seal tightly and store in the refrigerator for up to 3 days.

For the black olive tapenade:

1 Put all the ingredients into a food processor and blend until the olives are roughly chopped – not a smooth purée.

2 Spoon into cold sterilised jars and cover the top with a thin film of oil. Seal tightly and store in the refrigerator for up to 2 weeks.

For the green olive tapenade:

1 Put all the ingredients into a food processor and blend until the olives are roughly chopped – not a smooth purée.

2 Spoon into cold sterilised jars and cover the top with a thin film of oil. Seal tightly and store in the refrigerator for up to 1 week.

Fennel Vinegar

Prep and cook time: 10 min
Difficulty: easy
Makes: 600 ml | 21 fl oz |
  2½ cups vinegar

2 tbsp chopped fennel leaves
600 ml | 21 fl oz | 2½ cups white
  wine vinegar
1 tbsp fennel seeds

1 Gently crush the fennel
   leaves to release their flavour.

2 Put into a cold sterilised
   bottle or jar and pour in
   the vinegar. Seal tightly,
   shake well and leave to
   stand for 2 weeks, shaking
   occasionally.

3 Strain the vinegar into a
   cold sterilised bottle. Add
   the fennel seeds and shake
   well. Seal tightly.

Grandma's Note
The vinegar needs to stand
for 2 weeks to absorb the
flavour of the fennel.

Redcurrant Vinegar

Prep and cook time: 20 min
Standing: 72 h
Straining: 12 h
Difficulty: medium
Makes: 600 ml | 21 fl oz |
  2½ cups vinegar

450 g | 16 oz redcurrants
600 ml | 21 fl oz | 2½ cups white
  wine vinegar
white (granulated) sugar,
  see recipe

1 Crush the fruit in a large
  bowl and stir in the vinegar.
  Cover and leave to stand for
  3 days in the refrigerator,
  stirring frequently.

2 Ladle the fruit and juices into
  a scalded jelly bag. Strain the
  juice through the jelly bag
  overnight into a bowl. Do
  not squeeze the bag or the
  vinegar will be cloudy.

3 Measure the juice into a
  large heavy-based pan and to
  every 600 ml | 21 fl oz juice
  allow 225 g | 8 oz sugar.

4 Heat the juice and sugar in
  a pan and stir over a low
  heat until the sugar has
  dissolved completely. Bring
  to a boil and boil rapidly
  for 10 minutes, skimming
  off any scum.

5 Pour into hot sterilised bottles
  or jars. Cover, seal and label.

Blackberry Vinegar

Prep and cook time: 20 min
Standing: 72 h
Straining: 12 h
Difficulty: medium
Makes: 600 ml | 21 fl oz |
  2½ cups vinegar

450 g | 16 oz blackberries, plus
  extra to finish
600 ml | 21 fl oz | 2½ cups red
  wine vinegar
white (granulated) sugar,
  see recipe

1 Crush the fruit in a large bowl and stir in the vinegar.
  Cover and leave to stand for 3 days in the refrigerator,
  stirring frequently.

2 Ladle the fruit and juices into a scalded jelly bag. Strain the
  juice through the jelly bag overnight into a bowl. Do not
  squeeze the bag or the vinegar will be cloudy.

3 Measure the juice into a large heavy-based pan and to every
  600 ml | 21 fl oz juice allow 225 g | 8 oz sugar.

4 Heat the juice and sugar in a pan and stir over a low heat until
  the sugar has dissolved completely. Bring to a boil and boil
  rapidly for 5 minutes. Add the extra blackberries and simmer
  for 5 minutes. skimming off any scum.

5 Pour into hot sterilised bottles or jars. Cover, seal and label.

Walnut and Tomato Pesto

Prep and cook time: 20 min
Difficulty: easy
Makes: 250 g | 9 oz pesto

75 g | 2½ oz | ½ cup
   chopped walnuts
75 g | 2½ oz sundried tomatoes in
   oil, drained
2 cloves garlic, crushed
1 tbsp balsamic vinegar
salt and pepper
100 ml | 3½ fl oz | 7 tbsp extra
   virgin olive oil, plus extra
   to cover

1 Heat the oven to 180°C
   (160°C fan | 350°F | gas 4).
   Place the walnuts on a
   baking tray and put in the
   oven for 5–6 minutes until
   lightly toasted and golden.
   Set aside to cool.

2 Put all the ingredients
   except the olive oil in a food
   processor. Blend until
   smooth, scraping down the
   sides occasionally.

3 With the motor running,
   gradually pour in the olive
   oil until well blended.

4 Spoon into cold sterilised
   jars. Pour a little more oil
   over the top and seal tightly.
   Store in the refrigerator for
   up to 2 weeks.

Fresh Green Pesto

Prep and cook time: 15 min
Difficulty: easy
Makes: 250 g | 9 oz pesto

125 g | 4½ oz rocket (arugula)
  leaves, roughly chopped
50 g | 1¾ oz | ½ cup
  chopped walnuts
50 g | 1¾ oz | ½ cup grated
  Parmesan cheese
2 cloves garlic, finely chopped
sea salt
freshly ground pepper
80 ml | 3 fl oz | ⅓ cup extra virgin
  olive oil

1 Put the rocket (arugula),
walnuts, Parmesan, garlic
and a little salt and pepper
in a food processor. Blend
until smooth, scraping
down the sides occasionally.

2 With the motor running,
gradually pour in most of
the olive oil until well
blended.

3 Spoon into cold sterilised
jars. Pour a little of the
remaining oil over the top
and seal tightly. Store in
the refrigerator for up
to 1 month.

Pickles

On a hot day in Virginia, I know nothing more comforting than a fine spiced pickle, brought up trout-like from the sparkling depths of the aromatic jar below the stairs of Aunt Sally's cellar.

Thomas Jefferson (1743–1826)

Pickled Beets and
Picked Beans

Prep and cook time: 2 h 25 min
Difficulty: medium
Makes: 1 kg | 35 oz pickles

For the beets:
450 g | 16 oz beetroot
450 ml | 16 fl oz | 2 cups water
¾ tbsp salt
300–400 ml | 11–14 fl oz |
  1⅓–1⅔ cups white wine vinegar
1 bay leaf

For the beans:
675 g | 24 oz string (runner)
  beans, strings removed, sliced
water
1 pinch salt
600 ml | 21 fl oz | 2½ cups white
  wine vinegar
675 g | 24 oz | 3 cups white
  (granulated) sugar
1 tsp allspice berries
1 pinch pepper

For the pickled beets:

1 Heat the oven to 180°C (160°C fan | 350°F | gas 4).

2 Wrap the beetroot in foil and cook in the oven for about 1 hour until tender. Leave until cool enough to handle, then peel and slice the beetroot.

3 Heat the water and salt in a large pan and bring to a boil. Add the beetroot, reduce the heat and simmer gently for 10 minutes. Drain well.

4 Heat the vinegar in a pan with the bay leaf and bring to a boil.

5 Pack the beetroot into hot sterilised jars and pour over the boiling vinegar. Cover, seal and label.

For the pickled beans:

1 Put the beans into a pan and cover with water. Add the salt and bring to a boil. Cook for 8–10 minutes, until tender. Drain well.

2 Put the vinegar, sugar, allspice and pepper into a pan over a low heat and stir until the sugar has dissolved. Increase the heat and bring to a boil.

3 Add the beans and simmer for 5 minutes.

4 Pack the beans into hot sterilised jars and pour over the hot vinegar. Cover, seal and label.

Pickled Chilli Peppers

Prep and cook time: 35 min
Standing: 24 h
Difficulty: medium
Makes: 500 g | 18 oz pickled
  chillies

500 g | 18 oz red chillies
75 g | 2½ oz sea salt, for soaking
750 ml | 26 fl oz | 3 cups water
15 black peppercorns
5 bay leaves
2 tbsp coriander seeds
1 tbsp salt
6 tbsp white (granulated) sugar
1000 ml | 35 fl oz | 4 cups
  white wine vinegar

1 Slit open the chillies on one side only and remove the seeds. Place the chillies, sea salt and water in a bowl, stirring until the salt has dissolved. Cover and leave to stand for 24 hours. Drain, rinse and dry the chillies.

2 Put the remaining ingredients into a pan and heat gently, stirring, until the sugar has dissolved. Bring to a boil, then reduce the heat and simmer for 5 minutes. Remove from the heat.

3 Pack the chillies into hot sterilised jars and pour in the hot vinegar mixture, to cover the chillies. Cover and seal tightly. Store in a cool, dark place for 2 weeks before using.

Goat's Cheese with Lemon and Olives

Prep and cook time: 15 min
Standing: 24 h
Difficulty: easy
Makes: 1 kg | 35 oz cheese

2 lemons
sea salt
750 g | 26 oz fresh, firm goat's
   cheese, cubed
1 tsp whole black peppercorns
thyme sprigs
110 g | 4 oz green olives
750 ml | 26 fl oz | 3 cups extra
   virgin olive oil
150 ml | 5 fl oz | ⅔ cup walnut oil

1 Slice the lemons into about 8 segments each. Place the slices in a colander and sprinkle generously with salt. Leave to drain over a bowl for 24 hours, so that the lemon slices soften and lose their bitterness.

2 Rinse and dry the lemons then pack into cold sterilised jars with the cheese, peppercorns, thyme and olives.

3 Mix together the olive and walnut oils and pour into the jars, making sure the contents are completely covered.

4 Seal the jars tightly and store in the refrigerator. Eat within 1 month.

Pickled Salted Lemons

Prep and cook time: 720 h
Difficulty: easy
Makes: 600 g | 21 oz lemons

5 lemons, quartered
55 g | 2 oz | ¼ cup sea salt
3 cloves
½ tsp fennel seeds
4 black peppercorns
1 bay leaf
lemon juice

1 Sprinkle salt on the exposed lemon flesh.

2 Place 1 tablespoon salt on the bottom of a 600 ml | 21 fl oz jar. Pack in the lemons as tightly as possible, pushing them down, adding more salt and the spices between the layers.

3 Press the lemons down to release their juices and to make room for all the lemons. If the juice released from the squashed fruit does not cover them, add freshly squeezed lemon juice. Leave some air space at the top before sealing the jar.

4 Leave the lemons for 30 days in a warm place, shaking the jar from time to time to distribute the salt and juice. Rinse the lemons under running water before using.

Pickled Onions

Prep and cook time: 35 min
Standing: 12 h
Difficulty: easy
Makes: 1 kg | 35 oz pickles

1000 g | 35 oz small pickling
  onions or shallots, peeled
25 g | 1 oz salt
1000 ml | 35 fl oz | 4 cups white
  wine vinegar
2 tsp coriander seeds
2 tsp black peppercorns
2 tbsp white (granulated) sugar
  (optional)
bay leaves

1 Put the onions in a large bowl with the salt and mix together. Cover and leave overnight.

2 Rinse thoroughly in cold water and allow to dry as much as possible.

3 Pack the onions into cold sterilised jars.

4 Put the vinegar, spices and sugar (if using) into a pan and slowly bring to a boil over a low heat until the sugar has dissolved completely. Cook steadily for 15 minutes then remove from the heat and allow to become cold.

5 Pour the vinegar over the onions to cover completely. Tuck a few bay leaves into each jar, then cover and seal tightly.

6 Store in a cool, dark cupboard for 2 weeks before eating.

Chilli Peppers Stuffed with Goat's Cheese

Prep and cook time: 30 min
First standing: 12 h
Second standing: 8 h
Difficulty: medium
Makes: 900 g | 32 oz pickled chilli peppers

500 g | 18 oz large red chillies
250 ml | 9 fl oz | 1 cup
  white wine vinegar
25 ml | 1 fl oz | 5 tsp dry
  white wine
4 bay leaves
3 juniper berries
1 tsp chopped dried oregano
1 tsp black peppercorns
1 pinch salt
200 g | 7 oz goat's cheese
110 g | 4 oz olives in oil, drained
extra virgin olive oil

1 Cut the tops off the chillies with a sharp knife. Carefully remove the seeds and ribs.

2 Put the vinegar and wine in a pan with the spices, berries, herbs and salt and bring to a boil. Add the chillies and boil gently for 3 minutes. Drain (reserve the bay leaves, juniper berries and peppercorns) and place the chillies upside down on a cloth to dry overnight.

3 Beat the cheese until soft and spoon into the chillies with a teaspoon, pressing in the cheese to expel any air pockets.

4 Pack the chillies, reserved spices, berries and bay leaves, and olives into cold sterilised jars and pour in the oil to cover completely. Cover loosely and leave to stand for 8 hours. The chillies will absorb some of the oil and you will need to add more. Seal the jars tightly.

Pickled Vegetables

Prep and cook time: 25 min
Standing: 12 h
Cooling: 8 h
Difficulty: medium
Makes: 1 kg | 35 oz pickles

1000 g | 35 oz mixed vegetables,
  red capsicums (peppers),
  onions, cauliflower florets
sea salt
1000 ml | 35 fl oz | 4 cups
  white wine vinegar
4 bay leaves
8 cloves
1 tbsp peppercorns
1 tbsp coriander seeds
1 tbsp allspice berries
1 tbsp mustard seeds
2 sprigs flat leaf parsley

1 Slice the capsicums (peppers) and remove the seeds. Slice the onions.

2 Put the vegetables in a dish and sprinkle with a good layer of sea salt, weigh down with a plate and leave overnight.

3 Rinse the vegetables in cool running water and dry thoroughly.

4 Heat the vinegar with the bay leaves and spices and bring to a boil. Cook steadily for 10 minutes, adding the parsley for the last 2 minutes, then remove from the heat and leave to stand until cold.

5 Pack the vegetables in cold sterilised jars. Strain in the cold vinegar mixture ensuring that the vegetables are completely covered. Cover and seal tightly. Keep in a cool, dark place for at least 1 month before using. Once opened, keep in the refrigerator and use within 1 week.

Pickled Herrings

Prep and cook time: 40 min
Standing: 24 h
Cooling: 6 h
Difficulty: easy
Makes: 8 pickled herrings

8 herring fillets
200 g | 7 oz | 1 cup sea salt
1 pinch sugar
450 ml | 16 fl oz | 2 cups
   white wine vinegar
300 ml | 11 fl oz | 1⅓ cups water
250 g | 9 oz | 1⅛ cups white
   (granulated) sugar
14 allspice berries, crushed
14 black peppercorns, crushed
3 bay leaves
2 lemons, finely pared rind
3 chives, snipped

1 Place the herring fillets in a baking dish. Mix the salt with a pinch of sugar and cover the fish with the mixture. Cover and chill for 24 hours.

2 Heat the oven to 220°C (200°C fan | 425°F | gas 7).

3 Put the vinegar, water, sugar, spices and bay leaves in a pan. Stir until the sugar has dissolved.

4 Wipe the salt off the herring and discard. Add the fish to the pan and bring to a boil. Remove from the heat, add the lemon rind and pour the contents of the pan into a baking dish.

5 Cook in the oven for 20 minutes, cover and cool, then chill until cold. Discard the spices and bay leaves.

6 Put the herring and liquid into cold sterilised jars, making sure the fish is completely covered. Add the chives to the jars. Cover and seal tightly. Store in the refrigerator for up to 10 days.

Pickled Okra

Prep and cook time: 20 min
Standing: 12 h
Difficulty: easy
Makes: 1 kg | 35 oz pickled okra

700 g | 26 oz okra
1 tbsp sea salt
4 cloves garlic, halved
6–8 red chillies, split lengthwise
2 tsp coriander seeds
750 ml | 26 fl oz | 3 cups
   white wine vinegar
1 tbsp white (granulated) sugar

1 Put the okra into a colander over a large bowl and sprinkle with the salt. Cover and leave overnight to drain.

2 Rinse the okra, then press to squeeze out the excess moisture and dry with a cloth. Spread the okra on a cloth to dry thoroughly. Pack the okra and garlic into hot sterilised jars.

3 Put the chillies, coriander, vinegar and sugar into a pan and heat slowly, stirring until the sugar has dissolved. Bring to a boil and pour over the okra, making sure it is completely covered. Cover, seal and label the jars.

Pickled Fish

Prep and cook time: 35 min
Standing: 24 h
Cooling: 8 h
Difficulty: medium
Makes: 1 kg | 35 oz pickled fish

675 g | 24 oz fish fillets
1000 ml | 35 fl oz | 4 cups
  white wine vinegar
55 g | 2 oz sea salt, plus extra
  for the vegetables
2 cloves garlic
1 onion, thinly sliced
2 carrots, sliced
2 red chillies, sliced
225 g | 8 oz | 1 cup white
  (granulated) sugar
1 tbsp coriander seeds
3 tsp peppercorns
2 cloves
4 bay leaves

1 Put the fish fillets in a dish
   and pour over enough of the
   vinegar to ensure that the
   fish is totally submerged in
   the liquid. Add the salt and
   stir the mixture until the salt
   is completely dissolved.
   Cover and chill for 24 hours.

2 Put the garlic, onion and
   carrots into a dish. Sprinkle
   with a good layer of sea salt,
   weigh down with a plate
   and leave overnight.

3 Drain the vinegar from the
   fish and rinse the fish in
   cool running water. Rinse

the vegetables in the same
way. Dry the fish and
vegetables on a cloth.

4 Heat the remaining vinegar
   with the garlic, onion,
   carrots, chillies, sugar, spices
   and bay leaves in a large pan
   over a low heat until the
   sugar has dissolved. Increase
   the heat and bring to a boil,
   then lower the heat and

simmer for 5 minutes.
Leave to stand until cold.

5 Place the fish in cold
   sterilised jars. Spoon in the
   cold vinegar mixture and
   vegetables, ensuring that the
   fish and vegetables are
   completely covered. Cover
   and seal tightly. Store in the
   refrigerator and eat within
   1 month.

Pickles with Herbs and Spices

Prep and cook time: 15 min
Standing: 12 h
Difficulty: easy
*Makes: 450 g | 16 oz pickled
    cucumbers*

450 g | 16 oz small cucumbers
sea salt
700 ml | 25 fl oz | 3 cups
    white wine vinegar
3 bay leaves
6 black peppercorns
6 coriander seeds
6 allspice berries
2 cloves garlic, chopped
2 dill (dill weed) flower heads
4 sprigs dill (dill weed) leaves

1 Put the cucumbers in a shallow dish and cover with sea salt.
Leave to stand overnight, then drain and rinse well.

2 Put the vinegar, salt, bay leaves and spices in a pan and bring
to a boil. Boil for 10 minutes, then remove from the heat and
leave until cold.

3 Pack the cucumbers into cold sterilised glass jars, layering them
with the garlic and dill (dill weed) flower heads and leaves.

4 Strain the cold vinegar mixture through a sieve over the
cucumbers, making sure that the jars are filled.

5 Seal the jars and leave for 2 weeks before eating.

Pickled Eggs

Prep and cook time: 30 min
Difficulty: easy
Makes: 6 eggs

6 eggs
600 ml | 21 fl oz | 2½ cups white
  wine vinegar
6 peppercorns
2 cinnamon sticks
1 blade mace
1 tsp allspice berries
2 cloves
1 bay leaf
1 red onion, sliced

1 Boil the eggs for
   10 minutes, then plunge
   into cold water.

2 Put the vinegar, spices and
   bay leaf into a pan and
   bring to a boil. Boil for
   10 minutes, then remove
   the bay leaf, cinnamon
   sticks and mace.

3 Peel the eggs. Pack the eggs
   and onions loosely in a
   warm sterilised jar. Pour
   over the hot vinegar, cover
   and seal tightly.

Pickled Gherkins

Prep and cook time: 15 min
Standing: 12 h
Difficulty: easy
Makes: 450 g | 16 oz gherkins

450 g | 16 oz small gherkins
(dill pickles)
sea salt
700 ml | 25 fl oz | 3 cups white
wine vinegar
6 black peppercorns
6 allspice berries
1 blade mace
3 cloves
4–5 bay leaves

1 Put the gherkins (dill
   pickles) in a shallow dish
   and cover with sea salt.
   Leave to stand overnight,
   then drain and rinse well.

2 Put the vinegar, salt, spices
   and 2 bay leaves in a large
   pan and bring to a boil.
   Boil for 10 minutes, then
   remove from the heat, cover
   and leave until cold.

3 Pack the gherkins into cold
   sterilised glass jars with the
   remaining bay leaves.

4 Strain the cold vinegar
   mixture through a sieve
   over the gherkins, making
   sure that the jars are filled.

5 Seal the jars and leave for
   2 weeks before eating.

Pickled Red Cabbage, Apples and Cherries

Prep and cook time: 40 min
First standing: 12 h
Second standing: 9 h
Difficulty: medium
Makes: 1 kg | 35 oz pickled
    cabbage

1 red cabbage, shredded
3 tbsp sea salt
400 ml | 14 fl oz | 1⅔ cups
    cider vinegar
400 ml | 14 fl oz | 1⅔ cups
    red wine vinegar
2 bay leaves
1 cinnamon stick
1 tsp black peppercorns
2 tsp allspice berries
1 tbsp coriander seeds
5 cloves
2 tbsp white (granulated) sugar
2 cooking apples, peeled, cored
    and thickly sliced
225 g | 8 oz cherries, pitted

1 Put the red cabbage in a bowl with the salt and mix well.
Cover and leave to stand overnight.

2 Pour both vinegars into a pan and add the spices, seeds, berries
and leaves. Bring to a boil. Remove from the heat and leave to
stand for 1 hour.

3 Add the sugar to the vinegar and heat gently, stirring, until the
sugar has dissolved. Bring to a boil, add the apples and cherries
and cook steadily for 5 minutes. Cover and leave to stand
until cold (about 8 hours).

4 Rinse the cabbage thoroughly under cold running water and
dry well. Remove the apples and cherries from the vinegar
with a slotted spoon and layer with the cabbage in cold
sterilised jars.

5 Strain the cold vinegar over the cabbage, making sure the
apples, cherries and cabbage are completely covered.
Cover and seal tightly.

Weights & Measures

Oven Temperature

Celcius	Fahrenheit	Gas Mark
120	250	1
150	300	2
160	320	3
180	350	4
190	375	5
200	400	6
220	430	7
230	450	8
250	480	9

Liquid Measures

Cup	Metric	Imperial
¼ cup	63 ml	2 ¼ fl oz
½ cup	120 ml	4 fl oz
¾ cup	190 ml	7 fl oz
1 cup	250 ml	9 fl oz
1 ¾ cup	438 ml	15 ½ fl oz
2 cup	500 ml	18 fl oz
4 cup	1 litre	35 fl oz

Spoon	Metric	Imperial
¼ teaspoon	1.25 ml	1/25 fl oz
½ teaspoon	2.5 ml	1/12 fl oz
1 teaspoon	5 ml	1/6 fl oz
1 tablespoon	15 ml	½ fl oz

Weight Measures

Metric	Imprial
10 g	¼ oz
15 g	½ oz
20 g	¾ oz
25g	1 oz
55 g	2 oz
110 g	4 oz (¼ lb)
125 g	4 ½ oz
150 g	5 oz
175 g	6 oz
185 g	6 ½ oz
200 g	7 oz
225 g	8 oz (½ lb)
300 g	11 oz
330 g	11 ½ oz
370 g	13 oz
400 g	14 oz
425 g	15 oz
450 g	16 oz (1 lb)
500 g	18 oz (1 lb 2 oz)
600 g	21 oz (1 lb 5 oz)
650 g	23 oz (1 lb 7 oz)
750 g	26 oz (1 lb 10 ½ oz)
900 g	32 oz (2 lb)
1000 g (1 kg)	35 oz (3 lb 3 oz)
2000 g (2 kg)	71 oz (4 lb 7 oz)
3000 g (3 kg)	106 oz (6 lb 10 oz)
4000 g (4 kg)	141 oz (8 lb 13 oz)

Index

Aioli, Black and Green Tapenades 126
Apple and Celery Relish with Capers 109
Apple and Cranberry Jelly 52
Apple Blackberry Marmalade 13
Apple Chutney with Raisins 108
Apple Jelly with Chilli and Star Anise 42
Apple Vinegar 123
Apricot and Chilli Jam 32
Apricot and Plum Purée 105
Apricot Jam 22

Berry and Cherry Jam 21
Blackberry Jam 16
Blackberry Vinegar 130
Blackcurrant Jam 36
Blood Orange, Lime and Grapefruit Marmalades 26

Caper Tapenade 114
Carrot Jam 28
Cherry Compote 77
Chilli Jam 25
Chilli Jelly 54
Chilli Peppers Stuffed with Goat's Cheese 142
Crabapple Jelly 51
Cranberry Chutney 107
Cranberry Curd 65
Cranberry Jam 38

Eggplant with Thyme 86
Elderberry Jelly 67
Elderflower Jelly 57

Fennel Vinegar 128
Fig and Lemon Jam 20
Fig Preserve 88
Fresh Green Pesto 133
Fruit Mustard 78

Ginger Jelly 49
Goat's Cheese with Lemon and Olives 139
Gooseberry and Rose Petal Jelly 68
Gooseberry Jam 18
Green Apple Chutney with Ginger 102
Green Olives 76
Green Tomato Chutney 110

Kumquat Marmalade 12

Lemon Curd 44
Lime Chutney 98
Lime Curd 66

Mango and Ginger Chutney 106
Mango Jam 14
Mixed Fruit Chutney 100

Nectarine and Pineapple Jam 33

Olive Oil with Herbs and Lemon 115
Onion Chutney with Thyme 103
Orange, Almond and Apricot Jam 37
Orange and Lemon Jelly 50
Orange Curd 56
Orange Jelly 58
Orange Marmalade 10
Oranges and Peaches with Vanilla 80

Parsley and Walnut Pesto 116
Pear and Chocolate Jam 34
Pear Jelly 46
Pickled Beets and Pickled Beans 136
Pickled Chilli Peppers 138
Pickled Eggs 152
Pickled Fish 149
Pickled Garlic 89
Pickled Garlic with Rosemary 117

Pickled Gherkins 153
Pickled Herrings 146
Pickled Okra 148
Pickled Onions 141
Pickled Red Cabbage, Apples and Cherries 154
Pickled Salted Lemons 140
Pickled Vegetables 144
Pickles with Herbs and Spices 150
Pineapple Chutney with Chilli 92
Plum and Apple Jam 17
Plum and Walnut Jam 39
Plum Chutney 94
Plums in Red Wine 82
Pomegranate Jelly 61
Preserved Kumquats 83
Preserved Pears 72
Preserved Red Capsicums 75

Quince Compote with Vanilla 74
Quince Jam with Elderflower Syrup 31
Quince Jelly 62

Raspberry Jam 15
Raspberry Jelly 45
Red Chutney 104
Red Grape Jam 23
Redcurrant and Apple Jelly 47

Redcurrant, Cherry and Pear Jam 19
Redcurrant Vinegar 129
Rhubarb and Grape Jelly 64
Rose Hip Chutney 97
Rose Hip Jam 24
Rose Jelly 55
Rose Vinegar 122

Spiced Apple Jelly 48
Spicy Berry and Kiwifruit Relish with Chillies 95
Strawberry and Passionfruit Jam 35
Strawberry Jam 30
Strawberry Jelly with Green Pepper 60
Strawberry Vinegar 118
Sweet and Sour Pickled Onions 87
Sweetcorn Relish 101

Tarragon Oil 121
Thyme and Garlic Infused Oil 120
Tomato Chutney 96
Traditional Pesto 124

Vanilla Chestnuts 84

Walnut and Tomato Pesto 132
Watermelon Jam 29
Wild Garlic Pesto 125